Cas Clarke is a careers officer who wrote her first book, *Grub on a Grant*, after taking a degree in Urban Studies at Sussex University. She now lives in a rural retreat in Surrey with her husband and their mad cat and dog, Matti and Barney.

Also by Cas Clarke

Grub on a Grant
Peckish but Poor

Mean Beans

Cas Clarke

HEADLINE

First published in 1993
by HEADLINE BOOK PUBLISHING PLC

10 9 8 7 6 5 4 3 2 1

ISBN 0 7472 4233 X

Typeset by
Letterpart Limited, Reigate, Surrey

Printed and bound in Great Britain by
HarperCollins Manufacturing, Glasgow

HEADLINE BOOK PUBLISHING PLC
Headline House
79 Great Titchfield Street
London W1P 7FN

In loving memory of Debra
— the only other person
I know to have worked her
way through *Grub on a Grant*

Contents

Acknowledgements

During the writing of this book, my family received a terrible blow — the death of my dearly beloved sister. Without the loving support of my family and friends I would not have been able to finish this book.

However, my greatest debt is to my husband Andy, who whilst providing me with the love and emotional support I needed, also gave a great deal of practical help. For it is he who has been largely responsible for the typing of the manuscript. This was in conjunction with looking after the domestic arrangements, including the dog and cat — no mean feat! So to my darling husband my most loving thanks.

Introduction

This book is not aimed solely at 'vegetarians'. It is a book of vegetarian recipes. Of course you do not have to have taken the plunge and become a fully fledged vegetarian to enjoy eating vegetarian food. I know many people who have taken to eating mainly meatless meals but do not want to be tagged as 'vegetarians' — and why should they? After all, those who do eat meat are not tagged as 'meat-eaters'. No, my friends are perfectly normal people who just feel that they don't want to make a fuss about what type of food they eat, but have decided that on the whole vegetarian recipes tend to fulfil the guidelines on healthy eating. It is also useful to note that this type of cookery fits in well with today's lifestyle — you don't have to worry about using up meat or fish before it goes off. Therefore you don't have to rely on freezing food so often.

A point that I was asked to take into account when I announced that I was writing this book is shopping. My friends, like most of the populace, do the majority of their shopping in supermarkets — *not* in health stores. Therefore, they do not want a cookery book that uses ingredients 1) that they have never heard of and 2) that you have to make a special trip to the health store to buy. Like everybody else, they want a cookery book with ingredients that sound familiar to them and that they can obtain on their regular shopping trips. So in this book you will not find anything that cannot be bought in the majority of well-known supermarkets.

There are a number of vegetarian products on the market now that can be used as meat substitutes in vegetarian cookery. I am not yet convinced that this is what many people want from vegetarian cookery, although Linda McCartney does make quite a good case for them, and when trying out a number of the products from the range with her name I was impressed by some. On the whole, I have not used this type of product. However, for the adventurous I have included a recipe for beefless stew in which I used the beefless burgers from her range – and it is very good.

A product that I have used a few times is Quorn, not in its cubed state, but minced. Minced Quorn was actually launched whilst I was writing this book, and I have found it to be an excellent ingredient for quick meals. It does have two drawbacks, however. At the moment it is quite expensive – maybe if the sales go up it will come down in price. The other drawback is its appearance – I wonder if the manufacturers are aware that uncooked, it bears more than a passing resemblance to certain makes of cat litter! Perhaps they could change the colour . . . Whenever using minced Quorn, I tend to brown it quickly first, as I feel that this does a lot to improve its appearance. I would advise you to try it, as it really is a very good ingredient that takes on other flavours marvellously well.

When setting out this book, I decided that I would group the recipes together in chapters which would reflect the different types of cooking that the majority of us do. Therefore, you will find all the soups in one chapter, all the salads in another, etc. I have put together all those recipes which can be quickly made in a frying pan or wok under the heading Quick Fries – very handy for when you have returned home and must rustle up a meal quickly before you go out for the evening. And because my friends wanted a book that would appeal to those who are thinking about adapting to vegetarian cookery (or trying to persuade a partner to try it!), I have included some chapters which reflect the type of cooking we were brought up with – Bakes and Casseroles, Pies and Quiches. Easy recipes to start off with, that do not depart from the 'meat and two veg' formula – apart from not containing any meat!

I have not dedicated a special chapter to recipes that can be used when entertaining, but you will certainly find plenty of recipes that are special enough to be used for dinner parties. For starters, many of the recipes from On the Side could be used, and I have included two of my most popular dinner-party dessert dishes in Sweet Things. We do seem to be more aware of the health aspect of what we are eating nowadays. I recently looked through *Peckish but Poor*, and in the chapters dedicated to main meals I found that at least one-quarter of the recipes were vegetarian – a reflection, I think, that most people enjoy one or two meatless meals in their weekly cooking. However, I then looked at the chapter where I had collected together the dishes that my mother used to make, and the only vegetarian recipes here were for macaroni cheese and toasted cheese dishes. I think this shows just how our tastes are changing in this country!

In this book I have gathered together my favourite vegetarian recipes from *Grub on a Grant* and *Peckish but Poor*, but the majority are new recipes that I hope you will enjoy. If you have graduated from *Grub on a Grant* to this book, you may find that you come across recipes with similar names but that have themselves changed. This is because it is now some years since I wrote *Grub on a Grant*, and my style of cookery has evolved; I continuously change the way that I cook, incorporating new ingredients as they become available. I am sure that you will find this book as simple to follow as *Grub on a Grant*. I now have a husband that I get to 'trial-cook' my recipes. If he can cook them, anyone can!

Handy Hints

- The recipes in this book, like those in *Peckish but Poor*, are generally for two people. This is because I have found that most of my friends have only really started taking an interest in cooking when they have finally settled down with a spouse or live-in lover. However, it is very easy to halve the ingredients if you are cooking for one, or double them if you have friends coming round. A few of the recipes are for four servings – this is because these recipes are very good served cold as well as hot and can therefore be served the next day as well. In a couple of cases I suggest using two servings as a basis for another meal, e.g. my recipe for chilli sin carne is for four servings, so you could have chilli sin carne one day and then use the rest of the chilli in my recipe for chilli pie.

- Quantities of seasonings are given only as a guide; you will soon learn how to adjust them to suit yourself.

- Read the recipe CAREFULLY to ensure you understand it. Please pay attention to words such as 'gently simmer' – this means just that. If you go ahead and boil it, you will end up with a burnt pan and dried-up food! Also watch out for grilling on a 'medium' heat. Again, if you grill on high, you will probably end up with a burnt offering, or worse, a flash fire.

- When using beans in these recipes, I have generally stated the quantity of canned beans to use. It is much cheaper to buy dried beans and cook them yourself – if you have the time. If you are doing this, you need to start the night before you wish to use the beans. I use 4 oz (100g) of dried beans for two people. Soak them overnight in plenty of water. You must then boil them in *unsalted* water for 10 minutes, and then simmer for 30-50 minutes, depending on the type of bean you are using. (The specific time will be given on the packet.) Drain them, and then they are ready for use as specified in the recipe.

- Throughout the book I have used a standard conversion of 1 oz = 25g. For liquid measurements I use 1 fl oz = 25ml. These are not exact equivalents, so use one set of measurements or the other. Another useful piece of information is that 3 teaspoons = 1 tablespoon. (If you are halving 1 teaspoon of something because you are cooking for one, just a sprinkling, or dash if it is a liquid, will be sufficient.)

- Ovens vary enormously, but you will soon learn how yours behaves. If dishes start coming out overdone, turn the heat down by 10°C/25°F/Gas 1 whenever you cook, or similarly if dishes always take longer to cook than the recipe states, turn the heat up by the same amount.

Kitchen Utensils

You may have some kitchen utensils or may be in the process of starting to stock your new home. These are my suggestions for what will come in handiest.

A couple of large **chopping boards**.
Some good **sharp knives**. The most indispensable are a large chopping knife, a bread knife and a small knife with a serrated edge.
A couple of **medium saucepans with tight-fitting lids**.

It's a good idea to get a **steamer** which will fit one of these pans.

A small **saucepan/milkpan** for making sauces.

You will need some ovenproof dishes — I suggest a **casserole dish with tight-fitting lid**, a **gratin dish** and a **lasagne dish**, although if you can only afford one buy the lasagne dish.

Other bakeware should include a **baking tray**, 11 X 7 in (28 X 18 cm) **baking dish**, 8 in (20 cm) **flan tin**, 8 in (20 cm) **pie plate**, and for cakes 8 in (20 cm) **cake tins** and an 8 in (20 cm) **deep cake tin**. These should all be non-stick to keep life simple.

You can never have too many **wooden spoons**.

If you don't have a steamer, you will need a **colander**.

A **swivel-bladed potato peeler** is quick to use.

You will also need a **sieve**.

A **rolling pin** will be needed for pastry.

Absolute essentials in my book are a pair of **kitchen scales**, **measuring jug**, and **measuring spoons**.

For making cakes I would also say that an **electric beater** is essential; it really makes a huge difference in the amount of work you have to put in. If, however, you don't have one, you will also need a **whisk**.

For making soups and some sauces, a **blender/liquidiser** comes in very handy.

Ingredients

It seems that every week now new ingredients become available to us. In this book I have kept to products that are readily available from large supermarkets. However, if you cannot obtain certain seasonings, it is easy to substitute another. For many of the mixed seasonings that I suggest, you could substitute either chilli powder or a curry powder.

Here are my suggestions for items which you should keep stocked up on:

A couple of oils; my favourites are **olive oil** and **groundnut oil**. I always use **free-range eggs**, and, since I use a lot of garlic, I buy a **string of garlic** and keep it hanging on the wall. I love **butter** but also use a **low-fat soft sunflower margarine** which is suitable for baking. I keep both **self-raising** and **plain flour**, and a variety of sugars, the most commonly used ones being **soft brown**, **caster sugar** and **demerara**. It is useful to have a range of **pasta** and some **Parmesan cheese**. I tend to use a lot of **pesto, tomato purée** and **canned chopped tomatoes**.

I do use a lot of herbs and spices and I think you can get by with **Italian herbs, mixed herbs, paprika, chilli powder** and a medium **curry paste. Soy sauce** is essential and I also use a lot of **Tabasco sauce**. I often use **runny honey**. And last, but certainly not least, you will always find some **tomato ketchup** in my fridge!

There is now a range of pastes and purées such as chilli, garlic and ginger that can be substituted for the raw ingredient. With these new ingredients, all the work has been done for you, you just add them to recipes as required. In the text I often refer to these as 'lazy' chilli, garlic or ginger. Of course, you can always use the raw ingredient – I do prefer to prepare fresh garlic rather than use the 'lazy' version; it's completely up to you which you prefer to use.

1 Soups

Soups are incredibly versatile – and incredibly useful. If cooled after cooking they can be left in the refrigerator for 1- 2 days, as long as they are carefully reheated before serving. This makes them extremely useful, as they can be made ahead of time and reheated when necessary. This chapter is devoted to filling, nutritious soups which can be used as the basis for a main meal. I love to serve soups with grated cheese, chopped nuts, wholemeal or garlic bread or home-made croûtons. I also sometimes serve mustards and rouille (for which I have included a recipe on p. 163) which can be stirred into soups to intensify their flavour – or, if the flavour needs moderating, I serve yoghurt or sour cream, which people can use to vary the heat according to their own taste.

Obviously people's tastes do vary, and therefore the flavourings given here are only intended to be a guide. You should vary them to suit yourself. The thickness of a soup can also be varied by adding either more or less liquid. If you think that a soup is looking thicker than you would like (maybe your idea of a gentle simmer is different from mine!), you can always add more stock, water or milk.

NB: Some soups are better if liquidised or blended; I have marked these with an asterisk.

Creamy Onion Soup*
Serves 2

    1 oz (25g) butter
    2 onions, chopped
    2 medium potatoes, finely chopped
    1 pint (500ml) vegetable stock
    5 fl oz (125ml) Greek yoghurt
    salt and pepper
    sprinkling of mixed herbs

In a saucepan melt the butter and add the onions and potatoes, then put on a tight-fitting lid and 'sweat' gently for 10 minutes. Stir, then cook on a medium heat for a further 5 minutes. Add the stock, then bring to the boil and simmer for 10-15 minutes. Take off the heat and leave to cool slightly before adding yoghurt and blending. Season to taste, add herbs and reheat gently. Serve with grated cheese and crusty bread.

There are times when money is especially tight, and this is when good nutritious soups really come into their own. The next two recipes have been used time and time again in our house and are good examples of how easy it is to make simple soups.

Baked Bean Soup
Serves 2

> 1 onion, finely chopped
> 1 tablespoon (15ml) oil
> pinch of chilli or curry powder
> 1 tablespoon (15ml) tomato purée
> 16-oz (400-g) can baked beans
> 15 fl oz (375ml) vegetable stock

Fry onion in oil until soft, then add the rest of the ingredients and bring to the boil. Turn the heat down and simmer gently for 15 minutes. At this point you can thicken the soup by crushing some of the beans against the side of the saucepan. We love this soup served with garlic bread (see p. 164 for recipe).

Economical Soup
Serves 2

> 1 pint (500ml) water or vegetable stock
> 1 carrot, halved lengthways and sliced
> 1 leek, halved lengthways and sliced
> 1 potato, diced
> 8 oz (200g) any leftover cooked vegetables
> sprinkling of parsley

Put all the ingredients into a saucepan, bring to the boil and then simmer gently for 30-35 minutes or until vegetables are soft. Mash some of the vegetables against the side of the pan to help thicken the soup. Serve with grated cheese and wholemeal bread.

Spiced Coconut Soup*
Serves 2

> 1 onion, chopped
> 1 tablespoon (15ml) oil
> pinch of chilli ⎫
> pinch of ginger ⎭ or 1 teaspoon (5ml) curry powder
> 1 yellow pepper, finely chopped
> 2 oz (50g) split red lentils
> 10 fl oz (250ml) water
> 15 fl oz (375ml) coconut milk, made with 3 oz (75g)
>   creamed coconut

Fry the onion in oil until transparent, then stir in spices. Add pepper and lentils and stir well. Add water and bring to the boil, then turn the heat down and simmer gently for 15 minutes. To make the coconut milk, crumble the creamed coconut into a measuring jug, add enough hot water to bring to the 15 fl oz (375ml) measure, and stir well. Stir the coconut milk into the soup and continue to cook for 15 minutes. Remove from the heat and leave to cool slightly. Blend and then reheat gently. I usually serve this soup with poppadoms.

Red Lentil Soup
Serves 2

> 1 onion, chopped
> 1 tablespoon (15ml) oil
> 4 oz (100g) split red lentils
> 1 tablespoon (15ml) tomato purée
> 1 pint (500ml) water or vegetable stock
> 14-oz (400-g) can chopped tomatoes
> sprinkling of mixed herbs
> sprinkling of mushroom ketchup

Fry the onion in oil until transparent. Put in a saucepan with rest of ingredients. Bring to the boil and then simmer gently for 20 minutes. This is particularly good served with sour cream, grated cheese and tortilla chips.

Peppery Soup*
Serves 2

    1 onion, finely chopped
    1 clove garlic, crushed
    2 peppers of different colours, finely chopped
    2 tablespoons (30ml) oil
    14-oz (400-g) can chopped tomatoes
    2 tablespoons (30ml) tomato purée
    sprinkling of mixed herbs
    1 tablespoon (15ml) paprika
    15 fl oz (375ml) vegetable stock
    sour cream, to garnish

Fry onion, garlic and peppers in oil until soft. Add rest of ingredients except sour cream, bring to the boil, cover and simmer gently for 15 minutes. Remove from the heat and leave to cool slightly before blending. Reheat gently and serve with swirls of sour cream in the soup and tortilla chips on the side.

Pistou
Serves 2

    1 onion, chopped
    1 clove garlic, crushed
    8 oz (200g) carrot, diced
    1 green pepper, diced
    2 tablespoons (30ml) olive oil
    14-oz (400-g) can chopped tomatoes
    10 fl oz (250ml) vegetable stock
    2 oz (50g) small pasta shapes
    1 tablespoon (15ml) pesto

Cook onion, garlic, carrot and pepper in oil until soft. Add tomatoes and stock and bring to boil, then cover and simmer for 15 minutes. Add pasta shapes and cook for a further 10 minutes. Just before serving stir in the pesto. Serve this lovely soup with grated Emmental or Gruyère cheese and French bread.

Rich Mushroom Broth
Serves 2

1 onion, finely chopped
1 tablespoon (15ml) olive oil
8 oz (200g) browncap mushrooms, finely chopped
sprinkling of mixed herbs
extra pinch of thyme
2 tablespoons (30ml) tomato purée
1 tablespoon (15ml) chopped toasted hazelnuts
glass of red wine
1 pint (500ml) vegetable stock
chopped parsley, to garnish

Fry onion in oil until transparent. Add the mushrooms and fry for a few minutes until the juices begin to flow. Add rest of ingredients except the parsley, bring to the boil and then cover and simmer for 30 minutes. Garnish with the parsley and serve with a good wholemeal bread.

Cheese Soup
Serves 2

8 oz (200g) potato, finely diced
1 onion, finely chopped
1 carrot, finely diced
1 stick celery, finely sliced
1 pint (500ml) vegetable stock
1 tablespoon (15ml) chopped parsley
4 oz (100g) cheese, grated
2 tablespoons (30ml) single cream
black pepper

Put the vegetables, stock and parsley in a saucepan, bring to the boil, then cover and simmer gently for about 20 minutes or until vegetables are cooked. Add rest of ingredients and reheat until cheese has melted. Season to taste. This is particularly good served with crispy croûtons (see p.163) or chopped nuts.

The next two soups are particular favourites of mine. Not only are they very flavoursome, but they are also very good for you in that they are particularly high in fibre. The cannellini and tomato soup is especially useful when you are on a slimming diet and want a wholesome lunch, as it only has about 150 calories in it, yet contains about 10g fibre – which is a much better deal than you will get from most canned soups! However, for those who do not have to worry about the calories, this soup is made even better by swirling in some creamy Greek yoghurt just before serving.

Cannellini and Tomato Soup*
Serves 2

    14-oz (400-g) can passata (sieved tomatoes)
    16-oz (400-g) can cannellini beans, drained
    10 fl oz (250ml) vegetable stock
    1 tablespoon (15ml) basil
    salt and pepper

Place all ingredients in a saucepan and bring to the boil. Cover and simmer gently for 15 minutes. Remove from the heat and leave to cool slightly. Blend and then reheat gently. Season and taste before serving. This can be served with Greek yoghurt, grated cheese or chopped nuts, and wholemeal bread.

Brown Lentil and Tomato Soup
Serves 2

1 onion, chopped
1 clove garlic, crushed
1 tablespoon (15ml) olive oil
1 celery stick, chopped
1 carrot, finely chopped
1 red or orange pepper, finely chopped
1 small potato, finely diced
14-oz (400-g) can chopped tomatoes
4 oz (100g) brown lentils
1 pint (500ml) vegetable stock
pinch of nutmeg
pinch of curry powder
sprinkling of mixed herbs

Fry onion and garlic in oil until transparent. Place with all other ingredients in a saucepan. Bring to the boil, then cover and simmer gently for 40-45 minutes until lentils are cooked. Serve with crusty bread.

Parsnip and Apple Soup*
Serves 2

1 onion, chopped
2 tablespoons (30ml) oil
2 parsnips, diced
2 eating or 1 cooking apple, diced
1 teaspoon (5ml) curry powder or paste
1 pint (500ml) vegetable stock
5 fl oz (125ml) Greek yoghurt

Fry onion in oil until transparent. Add parsnips, apple and curry powder or paste and fry gently for 10 minutes. Add stock, bring to the boil, then cover and simmer for 30 minutes. Remove from the heat and leave to cool slightly. Blend and then reheat gently. Stir in yoghurt. This is another soup that is best served with poppadoms.

Vegetable Chowder
Serves 2

   1 onion, chopped
   2 tablespoons (30ml) oil
   8 oz (200g) cooked vegetables – I suggest carrots,
      broccoli, potatoes
   1 stick celery, finely sliced
   1 tablespoon (15ml) flour
   1 pint (500ml) milk
   1 bay leaf
   12-oz (300-g) can sweetcorn, drained
   black pepper, to season
   chopped parsley, to serve

Fry onion in oil until soft. Chop up whatever cooked vegetables you are using and add to onion with flour. Stir well and fry for 2 minutes. Add milk and the bay leaf, bring to the boil, then cover and simmer gently for 20 minutes. Five minutes before the end of cooking time, remove the bay leaf (if you can find it!) and add the drained sweetcorn. Before serving season with the black pepper and sprinkle with the parsley. I serve this soup with herb or mustard bread and grated cheese or chopped nuts.

I have named the following soup 'sticky soup' after the 'unctuousness' which comes from the okra!

Sticky Soup
Serves 2

> 1 onion, chopped
> 1 clove garlic, crushed
> 8 oz (200g) okra, chopped
> 1 tablespoon (15ml) oil
> 14-oz (400-g) can chopped tomatoes
> 2 tablespoons (30ml) tomato purée
> 10 fl oz (250ml) vegetable stock
> pinch of chilli
> chopped parsley, to garnish

Fry the onion, garlic and okra in oil until soft. Add rest of ingredients except the parsley and bring to the boil, then simmer gently for 20 minutes. Garnish with parsley and serve with crispy croûtons (see p. 163).

2 Salads

Salads obviously come into their own in the summer months. If we are having a good summer, you probably won't want to spend those precious summer evenings cooking in the kitchen. However, I often find that when cooking vegetarian meals at any time of year I prefer to serve a salad as an accompaniment rather than vegetables. Thus, in this chapter I have given recipes for salads which can stand alone as a main course, and for side salads. The main meal salads can be made in smaller portions and served on the side.

I have also included recipes for my favourite salad dressings. I am not a great lover of shop-bought salad dressings, although I do use shop-bought mayonnaise because I find that we do not use enough of it to justify making our own. When using mayonnaise, I often include other flavourings to add interest. It is all a matter of individual preferences, so go ahead and be creative – that's what cooking is all about.

MAIN MEAL SALADS

Eastern Fruit 'n' Veg Salad
Serves 2

> 4 oz (100g) carrots, cut into matchsticks
> 4 oz (100g) celeriac, cut into matchsticks
> 8 oz (200g) fresh pineapple, diced
> 1 small green pepper, diced
> 4 oz (100g) fresh beansprouts
> 2 oz (50g) unsalted peanuts
> satay dressing (see p. 32)
> grated coconut, to serve

After preparing all salad ingredients, combine in a large salad bowl and toss with the satay dressing. Serve sprinkled with grated coconut and a rice side salad.

Italian Salad
Serves 2

> 16-oz (400-g) can cannellini beans, drained
> 2 oz (50g) toasted flaked almonds
> 4 oz (100g) mushrooms, sliced
> 1 teaspoon (5ml) paprika
> 3 oz (75g) pasta bows, cooked
> creamy dressing (see p. 32)

Combine all salad ingredients together and toss with the creamy dressing. This is very good with a simple green side salad and some ciabatta bread. If you are an olive lover, you could serve a side dish of olives as well.

Easy Winter Salad
Serves 2

> 4 oz (100g) white cabbage, shredded
> 4 oz (100g) cauliflower florets
> 2 apples, diced
> 2 tablespoons (30ml) raisins
> 4 oz (100g) mixed shelled nuts
> 4 oz (100g) Edam cheese, diced
> mayonnaise

When you have prepared all salad ingredients, combine in a salad bowl and stir in the mayonnaise of your choice. Ensure all ingredients are coated with the mayonnaise. I like this with a crusty French bread.

Mixed Bean Salad
Serves 2

> 5 oz (125g) cooked butter beans ⎫ or 16-oz (400-g)
> 5 oz (125g) cooked red kidney beans ⎬ can mixed
> 4 oz (100g) cooked haricot beans ⎭ beans, drained
> 4 oz (100g) cooked French beans, sliced
> parsley and lemon dressing (see p. 32)

Combine all ingredients and leave for at least 30 minutes before serving. Serve with a rice salad and spinach side salad.

Mediterranean Salad
Serves 2

> 4 oz (100g) small courgettes, very thinly sliced
> 12 baby cherry tomatoes, halved
> 2 oz (50g) pitted black olives, halved
> parsley and lemon dressing (see p. 32)

In a shallow serving dish, arrange the courgettes and tomatoes. Position the olives evenly around the dish. Drizzle with the dressing and leave for 30 minutes before serving. I often serve this salad with some crusty French bread and a simple green salad.

Salad Ratatouille
Serves 2

> 1 onion, sliced
> 1 clove garlic, crushed
> 4 tablespoons (60ml) olive oil
> 1 aubergine, diced
> 1 green pepper, diced
> 1 medium courgette, diced
> 7-oz (200-g) can chopped tomatoes
> 1 tablespoon (15ml) pesto
> chopped parsley, to garnish

Pre-heat oven to 180°C/350°F/Gas 4. Fry the onion and garlic in half the oil for a few minutes. Transfer to a casserole dish and add other vegetables and the chopped tomatoes. Stir well and cook in pre-heated oven for 1 hour. Leave to cool. When cold, add the rest of the oil and the pesto. Sprinkle with the parsley. This is really wonderful with garlic bread.

Bean and Couscous Salad
Serves 2

> 8 oz (200g) couscous
> 1 pint (500ml) boiling water
> 8 oz (200g) cannellini beans, cooked
> 2 tablespoons (30ml) olive oil
> 2 tablespoons (30ml) lemon juice
> 2 cloves garlic, crushed
> 2 tablespoons (30ml) fresh parsley, chopped
> salt and pepper

Place the couscous in a saucepan and add the boiling water. Bring back to the boil, and then cover and simmer gently until water is absorbed by the couscous. This should take about 5-10 minutes. Leave to cool. Just before serving, stir in the other ingredients and season. This is very good with a fruity salad – I prefer a spinach and orange salad with it.

Green Lentil Salad with Mint
Serves 2

4 oz (100g) green lentils, cooked
5 fl oz (125ml) natural yoghurt
1 tablespoon (15ml) mint, chopped
1 tablespoon (15ml) lemon juice
1 clove garlic, crushed
small bunch spring onions, chopped
salt and pepper
coriander (optional)

Mix the lentils and yoghurt together and then stir in the other salad ingredients. Season to taste, adding coriander if you are using it. Serve with couscous or a rice salad and a plain green salad.

Mixed Cheese Salad
Serves 2

mixed lettuce leaves
2 celery sticks, sliced
1 eating apple, cored and cubed
3 oz (75g) Brie, cubed
3 oz (75g) Emmental, cubed
1 oz (25g) chopped walnuts
mustard vinaigrette (see p. 33) or walnut oil

Mix all of the salad ingredients together and then dress with the chosen dressing. I suggest serving this with French bread.

Crunchy Salad
Serves 2

> 1 bulb fennel, sliced
> 1 eating apple, cored and sliced
> small bunch of spring onions, sliced
> 2 tablespoons (30ml) sweetcorn kernels
> 8-oz (200-g) can red kidney beans, drained
> few crisp lettuce leaves
> French dressing (see p. 34)

Mix together the fennel, apple, spring onions, sweetcorn kernels and red kidney beans. Make a bed of lettuce leaves on each serving plate and pile the salad into the middle of the lettuce. Drizzle with French dressing just before serving.

This next dish is a particular favourite of mine. It is best made a day in advance, which helps the flavours develop wonderfully.

Cold Aubergine and Tomato Bake
Serves 2

1 onion, chopped
2 cloves garlic, crushed
olive oil
1 aubergine, cut lengthways and sliced
14-oz (400-g) can chopped tomatoes
2 tablespoons (30ml) tomato purée
salt and pepper
2 tablespoons (30ml) parsley, chopped

Pre-heat oven to 180°C/350°F/Gas 4. Fry the onion and garlic in some oil until soft. Transfer to a casserole dish. Fry the aubergine slices, a few at a time, transferring to the casserole dish as they brown – you will need quite a lot of oil for this. Then add all other ingredients to the casserole and stir well. Bake in the pre-heated oven for 40 minutes. Drizzle 2 tablespoons (30ml) oil over the casserole after it has cooled and before serving. This is heaven served with a green salad to which black olives have been added, and plenty of fresh, crusty French bread to mop up the juices.

Brown Lentil Salad
Serves 2

1 vegetable stock cube
4 oz (100g) brown lentils
lettuce leaves
3 tomatoes, chopped
1 cucumber, cubed
half a small onion, finely chopped
1 tablespoon (15ml) parsley, finely chopped
French dressing or mustard vinaigrette
(see p. 34 or p.33)

Fill a saucepan two-thirds full of water and add a vegetable stock cube. Bring to the boil and stir to dissolve stock cube; add lentils. Cook for 30-40 minutes — they will be soft but still retain their shape when done. Arrange the lettuce leaves on plates, then mix the tomatoes and cucumber together and place on the lettuce. Mix the onion and parsley with the drained lentils and dress with your chosen dressing. Add to the plates and serve immediately whilst lentils still warm.

SIDE SALADS

Rice Salad
Serves 2

> 4 oz (100g) long grain rice, cooked
> 2 oz (50g) pitted black olives, chopped
> 4 tomatoes, chopped
> parsley and lemon dressing (see p. 32)

Combine all salad ingredients and mix in salad dressing. Leave to stand for 30 minutes before serving.

Spinach and Orange Salad
Serves 2

> 4 oz (100g) small spinach leaves
> 4 clementines, peeled
> small bunch of spring onions, chopped
> Oriental dressing (see p. 33)

Put spinach leaves into a large serving bowl. Divide clementines into segments, add to the bowl, and sprinkle with the chopped onions. Add the dressing when ready to serve.

Coleslaw
Serves 2

> 2 oz (50g) white cabbage, thinly shredded
> 2 oz (50g) red cabbage, thinly shredded
> 2 oz (50g) carrots, thinly grated
> 5 fl oz (125ml) sour cream or Greek yoghurt
> 1 tablespoon (15ml) olive oil
> 1 tablespoon (15ml) lemon juice
> 2 tablespoons (30ml) mayonnaise
> pinch of mustard powder
> salt and pepper

Mix the vegetables together. Prepare the dressing by whisking together all the other ingredients. Combine with the vegetables and mix thoroughly.

Nutty Avocado Salad
Serves 2

> 1 avocado, ripe but still firm
> 1 tablespoon (15ml) pumpkin seeds
> 1 tablespoon (15ml) sunflower seeds
> 1 tablespoon (15ml) pine nuts
> French dressing (see p. 34)

Remove skin and stone from the avocado and slice thinly onto two side plates. Combine the seeds and nuts with the dressing and spoon over the avocado slices. Serve immediately.

Green Salad

Choose a few of the following ingredients to make a simple green salad. Mix with your chosen dressing just before serving. Simple oil dressings are often best, such as French dressing (p. 34) or chilli and tomato dressing (p. 33).

Choose from: cos or little gem lettuce, shredded
iceberg lettuce, thinly shredded
small young spinach leaves
watercress
cucumber, thinly sliced or chopped
green pepper, thinly sliced or diced
celery, thinly sliced
spring onions, chopped
fennel, thinly sliced
green dessert apple, thinly sliced or diced

Mixed Salad

For a mixed salad, take your basic green salad and add a few more ingredients from the following list. With a mixed salad I normally serve a flavoured mayonnaise or creamy dressing (p. 32).

Choose from: coloured lettuce leaves, lollo rosso, radicchio, etc.

different coloured peppers, thinly sliced or diced
radishes, left whole or sliced
red or white cabbage, thickly grated
carrot, thinly grated
tomatoes, halved or sliced
sweetcorn – kernels or baby cobs
nuts, chopped or halved
olives, chopped or halved
raisins or sultanas
mushrooms, sliced
celeriac, grated
courgettes, grated
sprinkling of seeds, e.g. sunflower, pumpkin, sesame

Nutty Spinach Salad
Serves 2

4 oz (100g) small spinach leaves
2 oz (50g) carrots, cut into matchsticks
1 oz (25g) chopped walnuts
1 tablespoon (15ml) groundnut or walnut oil
1 tablespoon (15ml) orange or grapefruit juice
salt and pepper
sprinkling of chives

Place the spinach and carrots in a large serving bowl. Gently heat the walnuts in the oil, remove from the heat and whisk in the juice. Season and mix into vegetables. Sprinkle with chives and serve immediately.

Potato Salad
Serves 2

>6 oz (150g) salad potatoes
>sprig of mint
>creamy dressing (see p. 32) or mayonnaise
>chopped chives or spring onions

Boil potatoes with mint for 15-20 minutes or until cooked and tender. Drain and mix with chosen dressing. Sprinkle with chives or spring onions and serve hot or leave to chill.

Indonesian Potato Salad
Serves 2

>6 oz (150g) salad potatoes
>satay dressing (see p. 32)
>3 tablespoons (45ml) Greek yoghurt
>sprinkling of fresh coriander

Boil potatoes for 15-20 minutes or until cooked and tender. Drain and mix well with the satay dressing and yoghurt. Sprinkle with coriander before serving.

Kidney Bean and Carrot Salad
Serves 2

>4 oz (100g) cooked red kidney beans
>1 large carrot, grated
>1 tablespoon (15ml) pumpkin seeds
>1 tablespoon (15ml) sunflower seeds
>1 tablespoon (15ml) pine nuts
>2 tablespoons (30ml) groundnut oil
>1 tablespoon (15ml) cider vinegar
>1 tablespoon (15ml) orange or grapefruit juice
>1 tablespoon (15ml) soy sauce
>1 teaspoon (5ml) wholegrain mustard

Mix together the beans, carrot, seeds and pine nuts. Then shake or whisk together the rest of the ingredients. Stir into the salad ingredients and leave to stand for 10 minutes before serving.

Indian Carrot Salad
Serves 2

    2 carrots, grated
    squeeze of lemon juice
    pinch salt
    1 tablespoon (15ml) black mustard seeds
    2 tablespoons (30ml) groundnut oil

Mix the carrots, lemon juice and salt together. Heat the mustard seeds in the oil until they 'pop'. Mix the oil and seeds with the carrots and serve immediately.

Rice and Mushroom Salad
Serves 2

    4 oz (100g) browncap mushrooms, sliced
    1 tablespoon (15ml) groundnut oil
    pinch of curry powder
    4 oz (100g) long grain rice, cooked
    Eastern dressing (see p. 34)

Fry mushrooms in oil until juices flow. Add curry powder and cook for 1 minute. Remove from heat and mix with cooked rice. When cool, mix with dressing.

SALAD DRESSINGS

Satay Dressing

2 tablespoons (30ml) crunchy peanut butter
1 tablespoon (15ml) soy sauce
3 tablespoons (45ml) groundnut oil
pinch of chilli powder
juice of half a lemon
black pepper

Put the peanut butter in a small bowl and gradually beat in the other ingredients until you have a smooth sauce.

Creamy Dressing

1 onion, finely diced
1 tablespoon (15ml) oil
1 tablespoon (15ml) mayonnaise
5 fl oz (125ml) sour cream or Greek yoghurt
sprinkling of tarragon

Fry the onion in the oil until soft. Cool and then mix with the other ingredients.

Parsley and Lemon Dressing

2 tablespoons (30ml) olive oil
1 tablespoon (15ml) lemon juice
1 tablespoon fresh parsley, chopped
1 clove garlic, crushed
1 teaspoon (5ml) caster sugar

Put all the ingredients into a container with a tight-fitting top and shake to mix.

Mustard Vinaigrette

3 tablespoons (45ml) olive oil
1 tablespoon (15ml) tarragon vinegar or sherry vinegar
1 teaspoon (5ml) mustard powder
1 teaspoon (5ml) caster sugar
salt and pepper

Put all ingredients into a container with a tight-fitting lid and shake to mix.

Oriental Dressing

2 tablespoons (30ml) tomato sauce
2 tablespoons (30ml) orange juice
1 tablespoon (15ml) soy sauce
1 clove garlic, crushed
pinch of ginger

Thoroughly whisk all ingredients together.

Chilli and Tomato Dressing

2 tablespoons (30ml) olive oil
1 tablespoon (15ml) red wine vinegar
1 tablespoon (15ml) tomato purée
1 teaspoon (5ml) chilli sauce
1 clove garlic, crushed
black pepper
pinch of sugar

Place all ingredients in a container with a tight-fitting lid and shake to mix.

Blue Cheese Dressing

2 oz (50g) blue cheese, crumbled
2 tablespoons (30ml) Greek yoghurt
2 tablespoons (30ml) milk
squeeze of lemon juice
salt and pepper

Thoroughly whisk all ingredients together.

Eastern Dressing

>3 tablespoons (45ml) groundnut oil
>1 tablespoon (15ml) cider vinegar
>1 tablespoon (15ml) orange juice
>1 teaspoon (5ml) caster sugar
>1 teaspoon (5ml) curry powder
>1 teaspoon (5ml) coriander

Place all ingredients in a container with a tight-fitting lid and shake thoroughly to mix.

French Dressing

>3 tablespoons (45ml) olive oil
>1 tablespoon (15ml) tarragon vinegar
>1 teaspoon (5ml) mustard powder
>1 teaspoon (5ml) caster sugar
>1 teaspoon (5ml) salt

Whisk or shake all ingredients together.

Wine Dressing

>4 tablespoons (60ml) olive oil
>2 tablespoons (30ml) white wine vinegar
>1 tablespoon (15ml) medium dry sherry
>1 tablespoon (15ml) caster sugar
>1 clove garlic, crushed
>pinch of mixed herbs
>sprinkling of Tabasco sauce
>salt and pepper

Put all ingredients in a container with a tight-fitting lid and shake together.

Mustardy Mayonnaise

>2 tablespoons (30ml) mayonnaise
>2 tablespoons (30ml) Greek yoghurt
>1 tablespoon (15ml) lemon juice
>2 teaspoons (10ml) French mustard

Whisk all ingredients together.

Garlicky Mayonnaise

    2 tablespoons (30ml) mayonnaise
    2 tablespoons (30ml) sour cream
    squeeze of lemon juice
    2 cloves garlic, crushed
    salt and black pepper

Whisk all ingredients together.

3 Bakes and Casseroles

I greatly enjoy bakes and casseroles. I think that one of
the reasons for this is that all of the work is done
beforehand, and I find it very satisfying just to be able to
take something straight out of the oven to the table. This
is why I often prefer these sorts of dishes when I
entertain, as it means I can spend time with my friends
enjoying myself, rather than in the kitchen, cooking.

As the emphasis here is on effortless cooking, as an
accompaniment to this sort of dish I tend to serve a salad
which can be thrown together at the last moment, or
new potatoes with another vegetable steamed over
them. Both of these options mean that very little time
needs to be spent in the kitchen at the last moment.
Many bakes and casseroles can be prepared and left in
an oven with a timer before you go to work, so that the
meal is ready when you return. If you have such an
oven, refer to the oven instructions to see how much
longer than the cooking time stated here you need to set
your timer for, to allow the oven to heat up.

Mean Beans
Serves 2

I have cooked these beans in a number of ways, but this is our favourite version. According to your own tastes you can add more sugar or garlic, or even more chilli – it depends how 'mean' you want them to be. I like to cool the dish slightly before adding the butter and serving. Or you can serve the butter separately, so that you can each add the amount of butter you like to the dish.

1 onion, chopped
2 cloves garlic, crushed
1 tablespoon (15ml) oil
16-oz (400-g) can cannellini beans, drained
1 tablespoon (15ml) muscovado sugar
1 tablespoon (15ml) red wine vinegar
1 tablespoon (15ml) treacle
1 tablespoon (15ml) golden syrup
1 tablespoon (15ml) wholegrain mustard
sprinkling of Tabasco sauce
1 teaspoon (5ml) 'lazy' chilli
5 fl oz (125ml) boiling water

'Mean Butter', to serve:
1 tablespoon (15ml) butter, softened
1 tablespoon (15ml) French mustard
1 tablespoon (15ml) parsley, chopped
1 clove garlic, crushed

Pre-heat oven to 180°C/350°F/Gas 4. Fry onion and 2 cloves of garlic in oil until browning. Add with rest of ingredients (except for those in mean butter) to casserole dish. Do not cover, and cook in a pre-heated oven for 1 hour. Just before serving, mix 'mean butter' ingredients together and stir into beans.

Beefless Stew
Serves 2

   8 shallots, quartered
   2 carrots, diced
   1 tablespoon (15ml) oil
   4 oz (100g) mushrooms, quartered
   knob of butter
   4 'beefless burgers', cubed
   glass of red wine
   1 tablespoon (15ml) cornflour, mixed to a soft paste
      with a little water
   5 fl oz (125ml) stock
   1 tablespoon (15ml) tomato purée
   1 tablespoon (15ml) mushroom ketchup
   1 bay leaf
   sprinkling of thyme

Pre-heat oven to 180°C/350°F/Gas 4. Cook shallots and carrots in oil until soft, add mushrooms and butter and cook for 5 minutes. Transfer with all other ingredients to a casserole dish. Cook in pre-heated oven for 30 minutes.

Bean and Broccoli Stew
Serves 2

    1 onion, chopped
    1 tablespoon (15ml) olive oil
    1 carrot, chopped
    4 oz (100g) mushrooms, chopped
    10 fl oz (250ml) Newcastle brown ale
    1 tablespoon (15ml) tomato purée
    2 teaspoons (10ml) cornflour
    1 tablespoon (10ml) chopped parsley
    sprinkling of thyme
    16-oz (400-g) can cannellini beans, drained
    12 oz (300g) broccoli florets

Pre-heat oven to 180°C/350°F/Gas 4. In a casserole dish, fry the onion in the oil until transparent. Add the carrot and fry for a few more minutes, then add the mushrooms and continue frying until the juices flow. Add the brown ale and tomato purée. Mix the cornflour with a little water and add to the casserole. Bring to the boil and then simmer until it starts to thicken. Add the rest of the ingredients and cook in pre-heated oven for 40 minutes.

Herby Bean and Cheese Bake
Serves 2

    1 onion, chopped
    1 clove garlic, crushed
    1 tablespoon (15ml) olive oil
    16-oz (400g) can butter beans, drained
    14-oz (400g) can chopped tomatoes
    2 oz (50g) thinly sliced Cheddar cheese
    fresh herbs of own choice, chopped (I prefer rosemary
      or basil, but parsley can be used)

Pre-heat oven to 200°C/400°F/Gas 6. Fry the onion and garlic in the oil until browning, then add, along with beans and tomatoes, to a casserole dish. Top with cheese and sprinkle with herbs. Bake in pre-heated oven for 30 minutes.

Baked Gnocchi with Mozzarella and Basil
Serves 2

> 2 portions potato gnocchi with tomato sauce
>   (see p. 137)
> 4 slices Mozzarella cheese
> fresh basil
> black pepper

Pre-heat oven to 190°C/375°F/Gas 5. Put the gnocchi with tomato sauce in an ovenproof dish and cover with sliced Mozzarella. Cut up or chop basil leaves and sprinkle on top of cheese. Season well with black pepper. Bake in pre-heated oven for 30 minutes until cheese has melted and gnocchi have warmed through. Serve with salad and garlic bread.

Moussaka
Serves 2

> 1 aubergine, sliced
> 2 tablespoons (30ml) olive oil
> 1 onion, chopped
> 1 clove garlic, crushed
> 8 oz (200g) minced Quorn
> sprinkling of oregano
> 14-oz (400-g) can chopped tomatoes
> 2 tablespoons (30ml) tomato purée
> 1 egg, beaten
> 5 fl oz (125ml) Greek yoghurt
> 3 oz (75g) cheese, grated

Pre-heat oven to 200°C/400°F/Gas 6. Fry the aubergine in half the oil, then put aside. Fry onion and garlic in remaining oil until soft. Add minced Quorn and brown. Add oregano, tomatoes and tomato purée. Put a layer of this sauce into a greased ovenproof dish, add a layer of aubergine, then continue with the layers, finishing with a layer of aubergine. Mix together the egg, yoghurt and cheese. Spoon over aubergine. Bake in pre-heated oven for 30 minutes. Serve with garlic bread and a tomato or green salad.

Swiss Potato Bake
Serves 2

>   12 oz (300g) baby new potatoes
>   2 oz (50g) Gruyère cheese, grated
>   2 oz (50g) Emmental cheese, grated
>   10 fl oz (250ml) double cream
>   1 clove garlic, crushed
>   salt and pepper

Pre-heat oven to 190°C/375°F/Gas 5. Boil potatoes for 15 minutes, drain and put in greased ovenproof dish. Mix half of cheeses into cream and garlic. Season. Cover with remaining cheeses. Bake in pre-heated oven for 45 minutes until browning.

Aubergines with Thyme
Serves 2

>   2 small or 1 large aubergine
>   olive oil
>   4 oz (100g) shallots, quartered
>   1 clove garlic, crushed
>   4 oz (100g) carrots, chopped
>   1 oz (25g) pine nuts
>   5 fl oz (125ml) cider
>   fresh thyme, chopped

Pre-heat oven to 180°C/350°F/Gas 4. Cut each aubergine into four, lengthways (eight, if using a large one). Then fry in olive oil until brown on all sides. Put aside. Fry the shallots, garlic and carrots in the oil until browned, then put in a casserole dish and place aubergines on top. Sprinkle with nuts and pour cider over. Add thyme. Cover and cook in pre-heated oven for 45 minutes.

Mediterranean Gratin
Serves 2

This is a particular favourite – both with us and with many of our friends. It is easy to double, or triple (!) the ingredients if making for larger numbers.

> 12 oz (300g) potatoes, cooked and sliced
> 5 oz (125g) Mozzarella cheese, thinly sliced
> 1 lb (400g) spinach, cleaned and cooked
> salt and pepper
> 2 tablespoons (30ml) tomato purée
> 3 tomatoes, sliced thinly
> 2 eggs, beaten
> 5 fl oz (125ml) single cream
> 2 teaspoons (10ml) red pesto

Pre-heat oven to 180°C/350°F/Gas 4. Into a greased casserole or lasagne dish put half of the potatoes, then half of the Mozzarella. Season the spinach with the salt and pepper and cover the cheese slices with it. Spread the tomato purée over the spinach. Cover with the remaining potato and then the sliced tomatoes. Mix together the eggs, cream and red pesto, pour over the other ingredients and cook for 35-45 minutes, until top is golden. Serve with a green salad.

Cheesy Pasta Bake
Serves 2

> 10 fl oz (250ml) cheese sauce (see p. 160)
> 2 oz (50g) sweetcorn
> 2 oz (50g) peas, cooked
> 6 oz (150g) pasta shapes, cooked
> salt and pepper
> 1 packet cheese and onion crisps
> 1 oz (50g) cheese, grated

Mix the cheese sauce, sweetcorn, peas and pasta, and season well. Put into an ovenproof dish and cover with the crisps and cheese. Grill under a medium heat until cheese is bubbling and topping is browning. Serve immediately with a crunchy salad.

Aubergine and Tomato Bake
Serves 2

> 1 onion, chopped
> 2 cloves garlic, crushed
> olive oil
> 1 aubergine, cut lengthways and sliced
> 14-oz (400-g) can chopped tomatoes
> 2 tablespoons (30ml) tomato purée
> salt and pepper
> 2 tablespoons (30ml) parsley, chopped

Pre-heat oven to 180°C/350°F/Gas 4. Fry the onion and garlic in some oil until soft, then transfer to an ovenproof dish. Fry the aubergine slices, a few at a time – you will need quite a lot of oil for this. As they are done, put the slices into the dish. Finally, add all other ingredients and 2 tablespoons (30ml) olive oil. Cook in pre-heated oven for 40 minutes. Leave until lukewarm and serve with garlic bread.

Aubergine and Tomato Gratin
Serves 2

2 aubergines, sliced lengthways
14-oz (400-g) can chopped tomatoes
2 tablespoons (30ml) tomato purée
1 tablespoon (15ml) pesto
1 beefsteak tomato, sliced
4 oz (100g) Mozzarella cheese, sliced
1 tablespoon (15ml) olive oil
black pepper

Pre-heat oven to 180°C/350°F/Gas 4. Put aubergine in a greased, shallow ovenproof dish. Mix together the chopped tomatoes, tomato purée and pesto, and spoon over aubergines. Arrange sliced tomato and Mozzarella on top and drizzle with oil, then season with black pepper. Bake in pre-heated oven for 35 minutes. Serve with garlic bread and a green salad.

Veggie Cassoulet
Serves 2

This is a really lovely dish and makes a very good choice for entertaining friends.

        1 onion, sliced
        2 cloves garlic, crushed
        2 tablespoons (30ml) olive oil
        14-oz (400-g) can chopped tomatoes
        2 tablespoons (30ml) tomato purée
        16-oz (400-g) can haricot beans, drained
        8-oz (200-g) can butter beans, drained
        4 oz (100g) browncap mushrooms, quartered
        1 tablespoon (15ml) molasses sugar
        1 tablespoon (15ml) herbes de Provence
        2 tablespoons (30ml) fresh wholemeal breadcrumbs
        1 tablespoon (15ml) Parmesan cheese

Pre-heat oven to 180°C/350°F/Gas 4. Fry the onion and garlic in the oil until soft. Put in a greased ovenproof dish with rest of ingredients except for breadcrumbs and Parmesan. Mix these two together and sprinkle over other ingredients. Bake in pre-heated oven for 45 minutes. Serve with garlic bread.

Pasta, Aubergine and Lentil Bake
Serves 2

        2 servings of aubergine and lentil sauce (see p. 137)
        6 oz (150g) pasta spirals, cooked
        7-oz (200-g) can chopped tomatoes
        black pepper
        2 tablespoons (30ml) wholemeal breadcrumbs
        1 tablespoon (15ml) Parmesan
        sprinkling of chopped parsley

Pre-heat oven to 180°C/350°F/Gas 4. Mix together the aubergine and lentil sauce with the pasta and tomatoes, and season with pepper. Put in a greased ovenproof dish and cover with breadcrumbs, Parmesan and parsley. Bake in pre-heated oven for 45 minutes. Serve with garlic bread.

Onion Bake

Serves 4

4 oz (100g) self-raising wholemeal flour
4 oz (100g) strong white flour
2 oz (50g) ground almonds
4 oz (100g) butter
2 tablespoons (30ml) oil
2 onions, chopped
8 oz (200g) fromage frais
3 eggs, beaten
2 tablespoons (30ml) milk
sprinkling of cayenne pepper

Pre-heat oven to 180°C/350°F/Gas 4. Mix together the flours and almonds. Rub in half of the butter. Stir in the oil and knead into a smooth dough. Roll out to fit an 8 in (20cm) flan tin. Prick base thoroughly with a fork. Put a layer of grease-proof paper in and then some coins. Bake in pre-heated oven for 10 minutes. Whilst that is cooking, fry onions in remaining butter. Mix the fromage frais, eggs and milk together. When the base is ready, remove greaseproof paper and coins. Spread the onions over the base and pour in fromage frais mixture. Sprinkle with cayenne. Put back into oven and continue to bake for a further 35 minutes, until golden brown and set. Serve hot with jacket potatoes and broccoli or cold with salad.

Tomato and Courgette Bake
Serves 4

> 1 lb (400g) tomatoes, sliced
> 1 lb (400g) courgettes, sliced
> 4 oz (100g) Mozzarella, grated
> 1 tablespoon (15ml) fresh basil, chopped
> 10 fl oz (250ml) whipping cream, slightly whipped
> 2 tablespoons (30ml) grated Parmesan

Pre-heat oven to 190°C/375°F/Gas 5. Put the tomatoes, courgettes and Mozzarella in a well-greased shallow oven-proof dish. Sprinkle with basil and pour cream over. Sprinkle with Parmesan and bake in pre-heated oven for 35 minutes. Serve hot with new potatoes and broccoli or cold with rice salad and a green salad.

Spicy Pepper Pot
Serves 2

You can make this dish a little less spicy by adding less chilli sauce – and the masochists among you can add more!

> 8 oz (200g) potatoes, cubed
> 4 oz (100g) carrots, cubed
> 4 oz (100g) leeks, sliced
> 1 each red, green and yellow pepper, chopped
> 1 pint (500ml) vegetable stock
> 14-oz (400-g) can chopped tomatoes
> 1 tablespoon (15ml) tomato purée
> 2 teaspoons (10ml) chilli sauce
> sprinkling of mixed herbs
> 2 tablespoons (30ml) paprika
> 16-oz (400-g) can flageolet beans, drained

Pre-heat oven to 180°C/350°F/Gas 4. Place all fresh vegetables in a casserole dish with the stock and bring to the boil. Cover and simmer for 20 minutes. Add all other ingredients and mix well. Remove a cupful of mixed vegetables and beans and liquidise, then return to the casserole (this will help to thicken it). Cook in pre-heated oven for 40 minutes.

Mushroom and Spinach Casserole
Serves 2

8 oz (200g) shallots, quartered
2 cloves garlic, crushed
2 tablespoons (30ml) olive oil
1 teaspoon (5ml) brown sugar
dash of vinegar
8 oz (200g) mushrooms, chopped
14-oz (400-g) can chopped tomatoes
12 oz (300g) frozen spinach, defrosted
glass of wine
salt and pepper

Pre-heat oven to 180°C/350°F/Gas 4. Cook shallots and garlic in oil until browning. Add sugar and vinegar and continue to cook until syrupy. Put this mixture with all other ingredients into a casserole dish and cook for 1 hour.

Nutty Mushroom Bake
Serves 2

8 oz (200g) mushrooms, sliced
3 tablespoons (45ml) olive oil
glass of red wine
1 clove garlic, crushed
1 onion, chopped
4 oz (100g) pine nuts, chopped
4 oz (100g) chopped mixed nuts
1 tablespoon (15ml) pesto
7-oz (200-g) can chopped tomatoes, drained
2 oz (50g) cheese, grated
salt and pepper

Pre-heat oven to 180°C/350°F/Gas 4. Fry mushrooms in 2 tablespoons (30ml) of oil until juices flow (approximately 4 minutes). Put into a casserole dish with red wine. Fry garlic and onion in remaining oil until brown. Add the nuts, pesto and tomatoes to the pan with half of the cheese and stir well. Spread over mushrooms and sprinkle with remaining cheese. Cook in pre-heated oven for 25 minutes.

Sweetcorn and Broccoli Bake
Serves 2

> 1 onion, chopped
> 1 clove garlic, crushed
> 1 tablespoon (15ml) oil
> 4 oz (100g) broccoli, cut into bite-sized florets
> 8-oz (200-g) can sweetcorn, drained
> 1 tablespoon (15ml) margarine
> 1 tablespoon (15ml) plain flour
> 5 fl oz (125ml) milk
> 2 oz (50g) Cheddar cheese, grated
> black pepper
> 8 oz (200g) creamed celeriac or potato

Pre-heat oven to 200°C/400°F/Gas 6. Cook the onion and garlic in oil until soft. Add broccoli and stir-fry for 2 minutes. Put this mixture into a casserole dish with the sweetcorn. Make cheese sauce with the margarine, flour, milk and Cheddar cheese (see p. 160 for method), and mix this in. Season with pepper. Place tablespoons of creamed celeriac or potato around sides of casserole dish. Cook in pre-heated oven for 30 minutes.

Courgette and Pepper Gratin
Serves 2

> 8 oz (200g) courgettes, grated
> 1 red pepper, diced
> 1 tablespoon (15ml) groundnut oil
> sprinkling mixed herbs
> 10 fl oz (250ml) cheese sauce (see p. 160)
> 2 eggs
> salt and pepper
> 2 oz (50g) Cheddar cheese, grated

Pre-heat oven to 190°C/375°F/Gas 5. Stir-fry the courgettes and pepper in oil for 2 minutes. Sprinkle with herbs and stir into sauce. Separate the eggs and stir egg yolks into courgette mixture. Whisk egg whites and add to mixture carefully. Season to taste and transfer to a casserole or soufflé dish. Sprinkle with cheese. Cook in pre-heated oven for 25-30 minutes.

Nutty Bean Crumble
Serves 2

1 onion, chopped
1 tablespoon (15ml) groundnut oil
8 oz (200g) boiled and sliced potatoes
8-oz (200-g) can baked beans
8-oz (200-g) can butter beans, drained
5 fl oz (125ml) cheese sauce (see p. 160)
2 oz (50g) chopped mixed nuts
2 oz (50g) fresh breadcrumbs
2 oz (50g) Cheddar cheese, grated

Pre-heat oven to 180°C/350°F/Gas 4. Cook onion in oil until browning. Layer into casserole dish with potatoes and beans. Cover with cheese sauce. Sprinkle with nuts and breadcrumbs, then sprinkle with cheese. Cook in pre-heated oven for 40 minutes.

Potato and Leek Gratin
Serves 2

> 8 oz (200g) boiled potatoes, sliced
> 8 oz (200g) leeks, sliced
> 3 oz (75g) Brie, sliced
> 5 fl oz (125ml) Greek yoghurt
> 3 tablespoons (45ml) double cream
> salt and pepper
> 1 oz (25g) fresh breadcrumbs
> 1 oz (25g) Cheddar cheese, grated
> sprinkling of paprika

Pre-heat oven to 180°C/350°F/Gas 4. Arrange layers of pot-atoes, leeks and Brie in a casserole dish. Mix together yoghurt and cream and season. Pour over vegetables and Brie. Top with breadcrumbs and Cheddar cheese and sprinkle with paprika. Cook in pre-heated oven for 40 minutes.

Cheesy Tomato Bake
Serves 2

> 16-oz (400-g) can butter beans, drained
> 12 oz (300g) cherry tomatoes, halved
> 5 fl oz (125 ml) whipping cream
> 1 oz (25g) Parmesan cheese, grated
> 1 oz (25g) Cheddar cheese, grated
> sprinkling of basil
> black pepper

Pre-heat oven to 190°C/375°F/Gas 5. Put the butter beans in the bottom of a casserole dish. Top with cherry tomatoes, skin-side down. If you prefer to use larger tomatoes, slice these and put in a layer over beans. Slightly whip the cream until just thickening, then mix with the rest of ingredients and pour over tomatoes. Bake in pre-heated oven for 35 minutes.

Orange and Butter Bean Casserole
Serves 2

> 1 onion, chopped
> 1 tablespoon (15ml) olive oil
> knob of butter
> vegetable stock cube
> 1 tablespoon (15ml) flour
> 15 fl oz (375ml) orange juice
> dash of chilli sauce
> sprinkling of rosemary
> 16-oz (400-g) can butter beans, drained
> 4 satsumas, peeled and segmented

Pre-heat oven to 180°C/350°F/Gas 4. Fry onion in oil and butter until soft. Crumble stock cube into frying pan and stir in the flour. Stir-fry for 2 minutes on a gentle heat. Gradually blend in the orange juice and then add chilli sauce and rosemary. Bring to the boil, then cook on a medium heat until sauce has been reduced by one-third. Put in a casserole dish with butter beans and satsumas. Bake in pre-heated oven for 30 minutes.

Creamy Vegetable Gratin
Serves 2

1 onion, chopped
1 tablespoon (15ml) olive oil
10 fl oz (250ml) cheese sauce (see p. 160)
5 fl oz (125ml) double cream
1 egg, beaten
2 tablespoons (30ml) fresh chopped parsley
1 tablespoon (15ml) basil
6 oz (150g) carrots, diced
8-oz (200-g) can sweetcorn, drained
5 oz (125g) leaf spinach
1 red pepper, diced
2 courgettes, diced
2 oz (50g) breadcrumbs
2 oz (50g) cheese, grated

Pre-heat oven to 200°C/400°F/Gas 6. Fry onion in oil until soft. Mix with cheese sauce, cream and egg. Place all the vegetables and herbs in a casserole dish and pour the sauce over. Sprinkle with breadcrumbs and cheese and cook in pre-heated oven for 30 minutes.

Peanut and Butter Bean Casserole
Serves 2

1 onion, chopped
2 cloves garlic, crushed
1 tablespoon (15ml) groundnut oil
14-oz (400-g) can chopped tomatoes
16-oz (400-g) can butter beans, drained
4 oz (100g) unsalted peanuts
5 fl oz (125ml) vegetable stock
2 tablespoons (30ml) peanut butter

Pre-heat oven to 180°C/350°F/Gas 4. Fry onion and garlic in oil until brown. Place in casserole dish with tomatoes, beans and peanuts. Blend stock into peanut butter and stir into casserole. Cook in pre-heated oven for 40 minutes.

Almond and Potato Casserole
Serves 2

    1 onion, chopped
    1 clove garlic, crushed
    1 tablespoon (15ml) olive oil
    6 oz (150g) salad potatoes
    4 oz (100g) carrots, diced
    6 oz (150g) broccoli florets, chopped
    10 fl oz (250ml) vegetable stock
    5 fl oz (125ml) Greek yoghurt
    1 tablespoon (15ml) ground almonds
    2 oz (50g) flaked toasted almonds

Pre-heat oven to 180°C/350°F/Gas 4. Fry onion and garlic in oil until brown. Add potatoes and carrots and fry for 5 minutes. Transfer to casserole dish, and add broccoli and vegetable stock. Cook in pre-heated oven for 45 minutes. Five minutes before the end of cooking time, mix together yoghurt and ground almonds and mix into casserole. Sprinkle with flaked almonds just before serving.

Chickpea and Sweetcorn Stew
Serves 2

    1 onion, chopped
    1 clove garlic, crushed
    1 tablespoon (15ml) olive oil
    14-oz (400-g) can chopped tomatoes
    16-oz (400-g) can chickpeas, drained
    8-oz (200-g) can sweetcorn, drained
    sprinkling of thyme

Pre-heat oven to 200°C/400°F/Gas 6. Fry onion and garlic in oil until brown. Transfer to casserole dish and mix in other ingredients. Cook in pre-heated oven for 35 minutes.

Barley Bake
Serves 2

1 onion, chopped
1 clove garlic, crushed
1 tablespoon (15ml) olive oil
4 oz (100g) pearl barley
14-oz (400-g) can chopped tomatoes
5 fl oz (125ml) sour cream
3 oz (75g) cheese, grated

Pre-heat oven to 180°C/350°F/Gas 4. Fry onion and garlic in oil. Add barley and stir-fry for 3 minutes. Put in a casserole dish with tomatoes and add enough boiling water to just cover. Cook in pre-heated oven for 40 minutes. Stir in sour cream and half of cheese, then sprinkle with remaining cheese. Turn oven up to 200°C/400°F/Gas 6 and cook for 15 minutes.

Lentil and Mushroom Bake
Serves 2

4 oz (100g) split red lentils
10 fl oz (250ml) water
1 onion, chopped
1 clove garlic, crushed
2 tablespoons (30ml) oil
1 tablespoon (15ml) tomato purée
sprinkling of basil
4 oz (100g) mushrooms, sliced
1 egg yolk, beaten
5 fl oz (125ml) Greek yoghurt
2 oz (50g) cheese, grated
black pepper

Pre-heat oven to 180°C/350°F/Gas 4. Cook lentils in water until they are soft and have absorbed all the water – about 20 minutes. Fry onion and garlic in 1 tablespoon oil until brown. Stir into lentils with tomato purée and basil. Transfer to casserole dish. Fry mushrooms in rest of oil until juices flow. Mix into lentils. Beat together egg yolk, Greek yoghurt and half of the cheese, then season. Pour over lentil mixture and sprinkle with the rest of the cheese. Cook in pre-heated oven for 35 minutes.

Aubergine Parmesan

Serves 2

> 1 medium aubergine, sliced
> olive oil
> 8 oz (200g) potatoes, boiled and sliced
> 10 fl oz (250ml) tomato sauce (see p. 139)
> sprinkling of basil
> salt and pepper
> 2 oz (50g) breadcrumbs
> 2 oz (50g) Parmesan, grated
> chopped parsley, to garnish

Pre-heat oven to 200°C/400°F/Gas 6. Fry aubergine a few slices at a time in oil until brown. Layer into a casserole dish with potatoes. Cover with tomato sauce and sprinkle with basil. Season. Mix breadcrumbs and Parmesan together and use to top casserole. Cook in pre-heated oven for 20 minutes and garnish with parsley.

Mediterranean Casserole

Serves 2

> 3 peppers of mixed colours, cut into chunks
> 4 cloves garlic, unsliced
> 1 onion, sliced
> 2 tablespoons (30ml) olive oil
> 7-oz (200-g) can chopped tomatoes
> pinch of sugar
> 1 tablespoon (15ml) parsley, chopped
> salt and pepper
> sprinkling of pitted black olives
> 2 oz (50g) pine nuts

Pre-heat oven to 180°C/350°F/Gas 4. Gently fry the peppers, garlic and onion in the oil until soft. Transfer to an ovenproof dish with tomatoes, sugar and parsley. Cook in pre-heated oven for 45 minutes. Just before serving, season and stir in olives and pine nuts.

Mushroom and Potato Hotpot
Serves 2

1 onion, chopped
1 tablespoon (15ml) oil
8 oz (200g) browncap mushrooms, quartered
knob of butter
14-oz (400-g) can chopped tomatoes
1 teaspoon (5ml) mushroom ketchup
1 teaspoon (5ml) muscovado sugar
sprinkling of Tabasco sauce
1 tablespoon (15ml) tomato purée
8 oz (200g) potatoes, cooked and sliced
melted butter

Pre-heat oven to 190°C/375°F/Gas 5. Cook onion in oil until brown. Add mushrooms and knob of butter and cook for 5 minutes. Add all other ingredients except potatoes and melted butter. Layer mushroom mixture and potatoes into an oven-proof dish, finishing with a layer of potatoes. Brush with melted butter. Bake in pre-heated oven for 30-35 minutes until brown.

Vegetable Crumble
Serves 2

4 oz (100g) cauliflower, diced
4 oz (100g) broccoli, diced
1 tablespoon (15ml) oil
12-oz (300-g) can sweetcorn, drained
1 courgette, sliced
10 fl oz (250ml) parsley sauce (see p. 160)
1 teaspoon (5ml) soy sauce
salt and pepper
2 oz (50g) butter
4 oz (100g) flour
2 tablespoons (30ml) rolled oats

Pre-heat oven to 190°C/375°F/Gas 5. Quickly stir-fry cauli-flower and broccoli for 3 minutes in oil. Transfer, together with sweetcorn, courgette, parsley sauce and soy sauce, to an ovenproof dish. Season. Rub the butter and flour together until the mixture resembles breadcrumbs, then mix in oats. Sprinkle this mixture over the bake. Cook in pre-heated oven for 30 minutes or until brown.

Tomato and Mushroom Bake
Serves 2

1 onion, finely chopped
4 slices wholemeal bread, crumbled
1 tablespoon (15ml) oil
knob of butter
2 oz (50g) chopped mixed nuts
1 tablespoon (15ml) chopped parsley
14-oz (200-g) can chopped tomatoes
6 oz (150g) mushrooms, chopped
salt and pepper

Pre-heat oven to 200°C/400°F/Gas 6. Fry the onion and breadcrumbs in the oil and butter, then mix with the nuts and parsley. Mix the tomatoes and mushrooms together and season well. Put half the breadcrumb mixture into a greased ovenproof dish. Cover with the tomato and mushroom mixture, sprinkle over the remaining breadcrumb mixture, and bake in a pre-heated oven for 30 minutes until brown on top. Serve with a watercress salad.

Beefless Cobbler
Serves 2

> 1 onion, chopped
> 2 tablespoons (30ml) oil
> 1 green pepper, chopped
> 10 oz (250g) minced Quorn
> 5 fl oz (125ml) vegetable stock or red wine
> 1 tablespoon (15ml) tomato purée
> 4 oz (100g) self-raising flour
> pinch salt
> 1 oz (25g) margarine
> 1 oz (25g) cheese, grated
> 4 tablespoons (60ml) milk

Pre-heat oven to 180°C/350°F/Gas 4. Fry the onion in oil, then transfer to an ovenproof dish. Fry the green pepper in the same oil and transfer to the dish. Fry the Quorn until brown. Add stock or wine and tomato purée. Simmer for 5 minutes and then transfer to the dish. Bake in pre-heated oven for 20 minutes. Rub together the flour, salt and margarine. Rub in cheese and then use milk to bind into a dough. Roll out and, using a scone cutter, make scones. Place these on surface of casserole. Turn oven heat up to 230°C/450°F/Gas 8, and cook for 10 minutes. Serve with a green vegetable or carrots.

Macaroni Cheese
Serves 2

> 4 oz (100g) quick cook macaroni
> 10 fl oz (250ml) cheese sauce (see p. 160)
> knob of butter
> 1 teaspoon (5ml) French mustard
> sprinkling of fresh breadcrumbs
> 1 oz (25g) Cheddar cheese, grated

Pre-heat oven to 200°C/400°F/Gas 6. Cook macaroni as directed on packet, then drain. Mix with cheese sauce, butter and mustard. Transfer to an ovenproof dish. Cover with breadcrumbs and grated cheese. Bake in pre-heated oven for 20 minutes. Serve with a tomato salad and garlic bread.

Bobotie
Serves 2

1 slice bread
5 fl oz (125ml) milk
1 onion, chopped
2 cloves garlic, crushed
1 green pepper, diced
2 tablespoons (30ml) oil
10 oz (250g) minced Quorn
1 tablespoon (15ml) medium curry paste
2 oz (50g) sultanas
2 tablespoons (30ml) mango chutney
1 egg, beaten

Pre-heat oven to 180°C/350°F/Gas 4. Soak the bread in the milk. Fry the onion, garlic and pepper in oil until soft. Add the minced Quorn and brown. Stir in the curry paste, sultanas and chutney. Remove the bread from the milk, squeezing out milk, and mix bread into the Quorn mixture. Put into a greased ovenproof dish. Beat the egg into the milk and pour over Quorn mixture. Bake in pre-heated oven for 40 minutes until brown on top. Serve with peas and carrots.

Ratatouille
Serves 4

2 tablespoons (30ml) olive oil
2 tablespoons (30ml) soft margarine or butter
1 aubergine, cubed
4 courgettes, cubed
8 oz (200g) mushrooms, quartered
1 onion, chopped
2 cloves garlic, crushed
salt and pepper
2 tablespoons (30ml) parsley, chopped
2 x 14-oz (2 x 400-g) cans chopped tomatoes
1 tablespoon (15ml) tomato purée

Pre-heat oven to 180°C/350°F/Gas 4. Heat oil and butter and quickly stir-fry all the vegetables. Put them with the rest of the ingredients into an ovenproof dish and cover tightly. Cook in pre-heated oven for 1 hour. Serve with rice or pasta. Can also be served with garlic bread, sour cream and grated cheese.

Cauliflower Cheese
Serves 2

1 cauliflower

Cheese Sauce:
1 oz (25g) butter
2 tablespoons (30ml) flour
10 fl oz (250ml) milk
5 oz (125g) cheese, grated
salt and pepper

Pre-heat oven to 220°C/425°F/Gas 7. Wash the cauliflower, and divide into florets. Cook in boiling salted water for 8 minutes. Drain. In a small saucepan, melt butter, and blend in flour. Cook for 1 minute, stirring continuously. Remove from the heat, and add milk slowly, stirring all the time. Return to the heat and bring slowly to the boil. Add 3 oz (75g) of the cheese, and season. Place cauliflower in casserole dish and pour cheese sauce over. Sprinkle with remaining cheese and bake in pre-heated oven for 15-20 minutes until browning on top.

4 Pies and Quiches

When you are first adapting to vegetarian cooking, pies and quiches are good recipes to start with, as you can serve them in the same way as meat-based recipes. Thus, you can still serve pies with accompanying vegetables, and salads with quiches. In fact, in many cases, if you are trying to introduce your partner to the idea of vegetarian cookery, there is a good chance that they will not even notice at first that no meat is involved!

Shortcrust Pastry
Makes 12 oz (300g)

> 8 oz (200g) flour
> pinch of salt
> 5 oz (125g) butter, chopped
> cold water

Put the flour, salt and butter into a bowl. Using your fingertips, rub the mixture between your fingers until it resembles fine breadcrumbs, then using a few tablespoons of water, mix to a dough. Only use as much water as is needed. Rest dough in fridge for 20 minutes before using. When rolling out, touch as little as possible and roll out on a floured surface using a rolling pin.

CHEESE PASTRY
Add 3 oz (75g) grated cheese and an egg yolk to the breadcrumb mixture. You will barely need any water at all to make this into a dough.

NUTTY PASTRY
Add 2 oz (50g) finely chopped nuts and an egg yolk to the breadcrumb mixture. Again you will only need about 1 tablespoon (15ml) water to make this dough.

POTATO PASTRY
Add 6 oz (150g) cooked and mashed potato to the bread-crumb mixture. You will only need 1 tablespoon (15ml) water to make this dough.

BAKING 'BLIND'
To use shortcrust pastry in quiches, you need to bake it 'blind'. Pre-heat oven to 190°C/375°F/Gas 5. Line an 8 in (20cm) flan tin with the pastry, then prick the base of the pastry all over with a fork. Put some greaseproof paper in the bottom, and weigh down with coins or ceramic beans. Cook in pre-heated oven for 15 minutes. Remove paper and coins before using.

Tarragon Tart
Serves 4

12 oz (300g) shortcrust pastry
3 eggs, beaten
5 fl oz (125ml) single cream
2 tablespoons (30ml) fresh tarragon, chopped
salt and pepper

Pre-heat oven to 190°C/375°F/Gas 5. Use the pastry to line an 8 in (20cm) flan tin. Bake 'blind' in a pre-heated oven for 15 minutes. Beat the other ingredients together and pour into the pastry case (remove the paper and coins first!). Bake for 20-25 minutes until the filling is set. This tart is lovely served hot with new potatoes and vegetables or cold with salad.

Walnut, Stilton and Broccoli Flan
Serves 4

12 oz (300g) shortcrust pastry
6 oz (150g) broccoli florets, cooked
4 eggs, beaten
10 fl oz (250ml) milk
5 fl oz (125ml) single cream
2 teaspoons (10ml) cornflour
black pepper
4 oz (100g) Stilton, crumbled
1 oz (25g) walnuts, chopped

Pre-heat oven to 190°C/375°F/Gas 5. Roll out the pastry and use to line an 8 in (20cm) flan dish. Bake 'blind' in pre-heated oven for 15 minutes, until pastry is cooked. Remove coins and greaseproof paper. Put broccoli into the bottom of the crust. Mix eggs, milk, cream and cornflour together, season with pepper, and pour this mixture over broccoli. Sprinkle Stilton into flan. Cook again on same heat for 15 minutes, then sprinkle with walnuts, and cook for a further 10 minutes. Serve hot or cold with salad.

Mushroom and Walnut Pie
Serves 2-4

> 1 onion, chopped
> 1 tablespoon (15ml) oil
> 8 oz (200g) browncap mushrooms, quartered
> knob of butter
> 1 teaspoon (5ml) mushroom ketchup
> 1 tablespoon (15ml) dry sherry
> 4 oz (100g) walnut halves
> 10 fl oz (250ml) white sauce (see p. 160)
> 1 tablespoon (15ml) double cream
> sprinkling of sage
> 6 oz (150g) nutty pastry (see p. 66)
> milk, to glaze

Pre-heat oven to 200°C/400°F/Gas 6. Fry onion in oil until soft. Add mushrooms and butter and cook for a further 5 minutes. Mix with all other ingredients except pastry and milk and place in a pie dish. Top with pastry, pressing edges down tightly. Cut two slits in the pastry top and glaze with milk. Bake in pre-heated oven for 25-30 minutes until brown.

Peanutty Pie
Serves 2-4

1 onion, chopped
1 clove garlic, crushed
2 tablespoons (30ml) groundnut oil
4 oz (100g) broccoli, diced
4 oz (100g) cauliflower, diced
4 oz (100g) unsalted peanuts, chopped
2 tablespoons (30ml) crunchy peanut butter
1 oz (50g) creamed coconut
1 teaspoon (5ml) soy sauce
boiling water
5 fl oz (125ml) vegetable stock
6 oz (150g) nutty pastry (see p. 66)
milk, to glaze

Pre-heat oven to 200°C/400°F/Gas 6. Fry onion and garlic in oil until soft. Add broccoli and cauliflower and stir-fry for 4 minutes. Transfer to a casserole dish with peanuts. Make peanut butter, creamed coconut and soy sauce into a smooth paste with some boiling water, add to vegetable stock and stir into vegetables. Top with pastry and press edges down firmly. Make two slits in the pastry top and glaze with milk. Bake in pre-heated oven for 25-30 minutes until brown.

Vegetable Pie
Serves 2-4

> 1 onion, chopped
> 1 carrot, diced
> 2 celery sticks, chopped
> 1 clove garlic, crushed
> 3 tablespoons (45ml) oil
> 8 oz (200g) browncap mushrooms, quartered
> knob of butter
> 2 tablespoons (30ml) parsley, chopped
> glass of dry white wine or cider
> black pepper
> 3 sheets filo pastry
> melted butter

Pre-heat oven to 190°C/375°F/Gas 5. Fry onion, carrot, celery and garlic in oil until soft. Add mushrooms and knob of butter and cook for a further 5 minutes. Mix with parsley and wine and season. Place in pie dish. Cover with filo pastry, brushing each sheet well with melted butter. Bake in pre-heated oven for 30-35 minutes until brown and crisp.

Homity Pies
Serves 2-4

> 12 oz (300g) shortcrust pastry (see p. 66)
> 2 onions, finely chopped
> 2 cloves garlic, crushed
> 2 tablespoons (30ml) oil
> 1 lb (400g) potatoes, cooked and mashed
> 1 tablespoon (15ml) margarine
> 1 tablespoon (15ml) parsley, chopped
> salt and pepper
> 4 oz (100g) cheese, grated
> salt and pepper

Pre-heat oven to 190°C/375°F/Gas 5. Use the pastry to line a four-hole Yorkshire pudding tin. Bake 'blind' for 15 minutes. Fry onions and garlic in oil until soft. Mix with potatoes, margarine and parsley. Season. Mix in half the cheese and pile mixture into pastry cases. Sprinkle with remainder of cheese. Bake in pre-heated oven for 20-25 minutes until golden.

Cheesy Butter Bean Pie
Serves 2

1 onion, chopped
2 carrots, diced
1 clove garlic, crushed
2 tablespoons (30ml) oil
5 fl oz (125ml) white sauce (see p. 160)
sprinkling of basil
sprinkling of sage
2 oz (50g) cheese, grated
16-oz (400-g) can butter beans, drained
2 sheets filo pastry
melted butter

Pre-heat oven to 200°C/400°F/Gas 6. Fry onion, carrots and garlic in oil until soft. Mix with all other ingredients except pastry and butter. Transfer to a pie dish. Cover with filo pastry, brushing each sheet with melted butter. Bake in pre-heated oven for 30 minutes until brown.

Spinach and Mushroom Pie
Serves 2-4

8 oz (200g) spinach, chopped
8 oz (200g) browncap mushrooms, quartered
2 tablespoons (30ml) margarine
4 oz (100g) Ricotta cheese
5 fl oz (125ml) single cream
salt and pepper
2 oz (50g) tortilla chips, crushed

Pre-heat oven to 180°C/350°F/Gas 4. Cook spinach and mushrooms in margarine for 5 minutes. Mix with Ricotta and cream and season well. Transfer to a pie dish and top with tortilla chips. Bake in pre-heated oven for 30 minutes.

Vegetable and Apple Pie
Serves 2-4

 1 onion, chopped
 2 courgettes, diced
 2 carrots, diced
 4 oz (100g) cauliflower, diced
 4 tablespoons (60ml) oil
 2 dessert apples, cored and sliced
 10 fl oz (250ml) white sauce (see p. 160)
 1 tablespoon (15ml) double cream
 2 tablespoons (30ml) cider
 sprinkling of chives
 4 oz (100g) white breadcrumbs
 2 tablespoons (30ml) mayonnaise
 2 oz (50g) cheese, grated

Pre-heat oven to 180°C/350°F/Gas 4. Fry vegetables in oil
until soft. Transfer with apples to a pie dish. Mix together the
white sauce, cream, cider and chives and pour onto vegetables. Mix breadcrumbs, mayonnaise and cheese together and
spoon over vegetables. Bake in pre-heated oven for 30-35
minutes until brown.

Borek
Serves 2

 2 oz (50g) Feta cheese, crumbled
 1 tablespoon (15ml) cottage cheese
 1 egg yolk, beaten
 sprinkling of mint, chopped
 2 sheets filo pastry
 melted butter

Pre-heat oven to 190°C/375°F/Gas 5. Mix together the
cheeses, egg yolk and mint. Cut each filo sheet into three
widthways. Divide cheese mixture into six even portions and
place each portion on a piece of filo. Fold pieces of filo into
little packages and brush with butter. Cook on a baking tray in
pre-heated oven for 12-15 minutes until crisp.

Undone Pie

Serves 2-4

1 onion, chopped
2 tablespoons (30ml) oil
2 dessert apples, cored and diced
12-oz (300-g) can sweetcorn, drained
10 fl oz (250ml) cheese sauce made with cider instead
   of milk (see p. 160)
6 oz (150g) cheese pastry (see p. 66)
milk, to glaze

Pre-heat oven to 190°C/375°F/Gas 5. Cook onion in oil until soft. Add apples and cook for 2 minutes. Mix with sweetcorn and cheese sauce and transfer to a pie dish. Top with pastry, pressing edges down firmly. Cut a cross into the pastry and fold edges back to reveal pie filling. Glaze with milk and bake in pre-heated oven for 35-40 minutes until brown.

Hashed Pie
Serves 2-4

> 1 onion, chopped
> 1 tablespoon (15ml) oil
> 12 oz (300g) potatoes, cooked and mashed
> 8 oz (200g) spring greens, cooked
> knob of butter
> 16-oz (400-g) can baked beans
> 6 oz (150g) cheese pastry (see p. 66)
> milk, to glaze

Pre-heat oven to 190°C/375°F/Gas 5. Fry onion in oil until soft. Mix with potatoes, greens, butter and beans. Transfer to a pie dish and top with pastry. Press edges down firmly and make two slits in the top. Glaze with milk and bake in pre-heated oven for 30 minutes until brown.

Spicy Bean Pie
Serves 2

> 2 carrots, diced
> 2 sticks celery, chopped
> 1 teaspoon (5ml) 'lazy' chilli
> 1 tablespoon (15ml) oil
> 16-oz (400-g) can beans in chilli sauce
> 8-oz (200-g) can butter beans, drained
> 1 tablespoon (15ml) margarine
> 1 tablespoon (15ml) wholegrain mustard
> 1 oz (25g) cheese, grated
> 6 slices French bread

Pre-heat oven to 200°C/400°F/Gas 6. Fry carrots, celery and chilli in oil until soft. Mix with beans and transfer to a pie dish. Mix margarine, mustard and cheese together and spread over bread slices. Place bread (cheese side up) on top of bean mixture. Bake in pre-heated oven for 25-30 minutes until cheese is bubbling.

Spinach and Cheese Pie
Serves 2-4

  1 onion, chopped
  1 clove garlic, crushed
  2 tablespoons (30ml) oil
  12 oz (300g) fresh spinach, chopped
  4 oz (100g) Feta cheese, crumbled
  2 eggs, beaten
  black pepper
  pinch of nutmeg
  8 sheets filo pastry
  melted butter

Pre-heat oven to 190°C/375°F/Gas 5. Fry onion and garlic in oil until soft. Add spinach and cook for 5 minutes. Remove from heat and stir into cheese and eggs. Season with pepper and nutmeg. In an 8 in (20cm) flan dish, layer four sheets of filo pastry, brushing each with melted butter. Leave a little of each sheet overlapping the sides of the dish. Fill with cheese mixture and fold filo over mixture. Cover with remaining filo, folding overlapping pastry down into sides of dish. Brush with more melted butter and bake in pre-heated oven for 45 minutes until filo is puffy and brown.

Shepherdess Pie
Serves 2

4 oz (100g) split red lentils
15 fl oz (375ml) boiling water
1 onion, chopped
2 carrots, diced
1 tablespoon (15ml) oil
1 teaspoon (5ml) mushroom ketchup
1 teaspoon (5ml) gravy browning
1 tablespoon (15ml) cornflour
10 fl oz (250ml) vegetable stock
sprinkling of chives, chopped
sprinkling of parsley, chopped
salt and pepper
1 lb (400g) potatoes, cooked and mashed
1 tablespoon (15ml) margarine

Pre-heat oven to 200°C/400°F/Gas 6. Cook lentils in boiling water until all water is absorbed. Fry onion and carrots in oil until browning. Add cooked lentils, mushroom ketchup and gravy browning. Stir in cornflour and slowly blend in stock. Add herbs and season. Transfer to a pie dish. Mix mash with margarine and use to top pie. Bake in pre-heated oven for 25 minutes until browning.

COTTAGE PIE
Follow the recipe above, but add 3 oz (75g) grated cheese to the mashed potato.

Macaroni-topped Pie
Serves 2

> 2 portions ratatouille (see p. 22)
> 1 tablespoon (15ml) red pesto
> 1 teaspoon (5ml) sugar
> 5 fl oz (125ml) milk
> 2 teaspoons (10ml) cornflour
> 4 oz (100g) Mozzarella cheese, grated
> salt and pepper
> 4 oz (100g) macaroni, cooked
> 1 tablespoon (15ml) Parmesan cheese, grated

Pre-heat oven to 200°C/400°F/Gas 6. Heat ratatouille with pesto and sugar and transfer to a pie dish. Using a little of the milk, make a paste with the cornflour. Heat remaining milk, add to cornflour, return to heat and stir until it thickens. Mix with Mozzarella and season, then mix in macaroni and use to top pie. Sprinkle with Parmesan and bake in pre-heated oven for 25-30 minutes until brown.

Corn and Potato Pie
Serves 2

12-oz (300-g) can sweetcorn, drained
10 fl oz (250ml) cheese sauce (see p. 160)
pinch of mustard powder
8 oz (200g) cooked potatoes, sliced
salt and pepper
2 tablespoons (30ml) chopped nuts
2 tablespoons (30ml) breadcrumbs
2 tablespoons (30ml) cheese, grated

Pre-heat oven to 180°C/350°F/Gas 4. Mix together the sweetcorn, cheese sauce and mustard powder. Layer alternately with the potatoes into a pie dish, seasoning each layer. Mix rest of ingredients together and use to top pie. Bake in preheated oven for 30-35 minutes.

Chilli Pie
Serves 2

2 servings chilli sin carne (see p. 120)
1 sheet bought puff pastry

Pre-heat oven to 220°C/425°F/Gas 7. Put chilli sin carne into a pie dish. Cover with puff pastry, trimming edges. Bake in pre-heated oven for 25 minutes. Serve with a green vegetable.

Ratpie
Serves 2

2 portions ratatouille (see p. 22)
sprinkling of herbes de Provence
2 oz (50g) cheese, grated
12 oz (300g) cheese or nutty pastry (see p. 66)
milk, to glaze
sesame seeds

Pre-heat oven to 200°C/400°F/Gas 6. Put ratatouille into a pie dish and mix in herbs. Sprinkle with cheese, then cover with pastry (use any extra pastry to decorate). Make two slits in top of pastry, brush with milk and sprinkle with sesame seeds. Bake in pre-heated oven for 35 minutes until pastry is brown and cooked. Serve with salad or broccoli.

Lentil Quiche
Serves 2-4

> 6 oz (150g) red split lentils
> boiling water
> 1 onion, chopped
> 1 clove garlic, crushed
> 2 tablespoons (30ml) oil
> 1 tablespoon (15ml) tomato purée
> 2 tablespoons (30ml) double cream
> 2 eggs, beaten
> sprinkling of chives, chopped
> 2 oz (50g) cheese, grated
> 12 oz (300g) pastry case, baked 'blind' (see p. 66)

Pre-heat oven to 190°C/375°F/Gas 5. Cook lentils in boiling water for 10 minutes, then drain. Fry onion and garlic in oil until soft. Mix with lentils, tomato purée, cream, eggs, chives and half of cheese. Spoon into pastry case. Sprinkle with remaining cheese. Bake in pre-heated oven for 35-40 minutes.

Asparagus Quiche
Serves 2-4

> 8 oz (200g) cooked asparagus, chopped
> 12 oz (300g) pastry case, 'baked blind' (see p. 66)
> 5 fl oz (125ml) single cream
> 2 eggs, beaten
> 1 oz (25g) cheese, grated
> salt and pepper

Pre-heat oven to 190°C/375°F/Gas 5. Place asparagus in pastry case. Mix all other ingredients together and spoon on top of asparagus. Bake in pre-heated oven for 35-40 minutes.

Broccoli and Pepper Quiche
Serves 2-4

1 red pepper, diced
6 oz (150g) broccoli, diced
1 tablespoon (15ml) oil
2 oz (50g) Ricotta cheese
3 fl oz (75ml) single cream
2 eggs, beaten
sprinkling of oregano
salt and pepper
12 oz (300g) pastry case, baked 'blind' (see p. 66)
2 tablespoons (30ml) cheese, grated

Pre-heat oven to 190°C/375°F/Gas 5. Cook pepper and broccoli for 4 minutes in oil. Mix with Ricotta cheese, cream, eggs and oregano, season and spoon into pastry case. Sprinkle with cheese and bake in pre-heated oven for 35-40 minutes.

Pear and Stilton Quiche
Serves 2-4

4 tinned pear halves, sliced
12 oz (300g) pastry case, baked 'blind' (see p. 66)
4 oz (100g) Stilton, crumbled
3 fl oz (75ml) single cream
2 eggs, beaten
salt and pepper

Pre-heat oven to 190°C/375°F/Gas 5. Place the pear slices into the pastry case and sprinkle with the Stilton. Beat together the cream and eggs and season. Spoon onto the pears and Stilton. Bake in pre-heated oven for 35-40 minutes.

Blue Cheese Quiche
Serves 2-4

> 4 oz (100g) blue cheese
> 6 oz (150g) cream cheese
> 5 fl oz (125ml) single cream
> 2 eggs, beaten
> pinch of mustard powder
> sprinkling of chives, chopped
> salt and pepper
> 12 oz (300g) pastry case, baked 'blind' (see p. 66)

Pre-heat oven to 190°C/375°F/Gas 5. Mix all ingredients except for pastry case together. Spoon into pastry case. Bake in pre-heated oven for 35-40 minutes.

Minted Pea Quiche
Serves 2-4

> 8 oz (200g) cooked peas
> 2 tablespoons (30ml) mint, chopped
> few spring onions, chopped
> 12 oz (300g) pastry case, baked 'blind' (see p. 66)
> 5 fl oz (125ml) double cream
> 1 large egg, beaten
> salt and pepper

Pre-heat oven to 190°C/375°F/Gas 5. Place peas, mint and onions in pastry case. Beat the cream and egg together, season and spoon into the quiche. Bake in pre-heated oven for 35-40 minutes.

Mushroom and Leek Quiche
Serves 2-4

4 oz (100g) mushrooms, sliced
1 leek, sliced
knob of butter
12 oz (300g) pastry case, baked 'blind' (see p. 66)
5 fl oz (125ml) single cream
2 large eggs, beaten
1 oz (25g) cheese, grated
pinch of sage

Pre-heat oven to 190°C/375°F/Gas 5. Fry the mushrooms and leek in the butter until soft. Put into pastry case. Beat all other ingredients together and spoon over vegetables. Bake in pre-heated oven for 30-35 minutes.

Onion Quiche
Serves 2-4

2 onions, sliced
12 oz (300g) pastry base, baked 'blind' (see p. 66)
2 tablespoons (30ml) oil
6 oz (150g) fromage frais
2 eggs, beaten
salt and pepper
pinch of mustard powder

Pre-heat oven to 190°C/375°F/Gas 5. Fry onions in oil until brown. Place in pastry case. Beat all other ingredients together and spoon into pastry case. Bake in pre-heated oven for 35-40 minutes.

Sweetcorn Quiche
Serves 2-4

> 8-oz (200-g) can sweetcorn, drained
> few spring onions, chopped
> 1 tablespoon (15ml) parsley, chopped
> 12 oz (300g) pastry case, baked 'blind' (see p. 66)
> 5 fl oz (125ml) single cream
> 2 eggs, beaten
> salt and pepper

Pre-heat oven to 190°C/375°F/Gas 5. Put sweetcorn, onions and parsley into pastry case. Beat rest of ingredients together and spoon into pastry case. Bake in pre-heated oven for 35-40 minutes.

Courgette Quiche
Serves 2-4

> 1 courgette, thickly sliced
> boiling water
> 12 oz (300g) pastry case, baked 'blind' (see p. 66)
> 5 fl oz (125ml) double cream
> 2 eggs, beaten
> sprinkling of chives, chopped
> salt and pepper
> 2 oz (50g) cheese, grated

Pre-heat oven to 190°C/375°F/Gas 5. Blanch courgette slices in boiling water for 1 minute. Place up-ended in pastry case. Beat rest of ingredients together and spoon into case. Bake in pre-heated oven for 35-40 minutes.

5 Roasts 'n' Stuffs

For many people, these are the backbone of vegetarian cookery. If you become 'tagged' as a vegetarian, there is a good chance that when you are being entertained by friends you will often be offered nut roasts or stuffed vegetables as your main course. In fact I believe that many vegetarians have become heartily sick of nut roast! However, for those of you who are just embarking on a vegetarian diet I have given some of my favourite roasts – including my recipe for stuffed nut roast, which I have often used when entertaining. No one has actually complained 'Not nut roast again' to me yet!

Mushroom Stuffed Pasties
Serves 2

1 onion, chopped
1 clove garlic, crushed
1 tablespoon (15ml) oil
4 oz (100g) mushrooms, diced
knob of butter
1 teaspoon (5ml) mushroom ketchup
1 teaspoon (5ml) tomato purée
salt and pepper
8 oz (200g) bought flaky pastry
milk, to glaze

Pre-heat oven to 220°C/425°F/Gas 7. Fry onion and garlic in oil until soft. Add mushrooms and butter and cook for a further 5 minutes. Add mushroom ketchup, tomato purée and seasoning. Mix well. Divide pastry up into 2 balls. Roll each out into an 8 in (20cm) circle. Divide mixture between circles. For each circle, fold one side over the mixture and seal edges, crimping them together. Brush with milk and cook in pre-heated oven on a baking tray for 25-30 minutes until pastry is brown and well risen. These make an excellent lunch or late supper.

Carrot and Lentil Roast
Serves 4

1 onion, chopped
1 clove garlic, crushed
1 tablespoon (15ml) oil
8 oz (200g) red split lentils
15 fl oz (375ml) vegetable stock
4 carrots, grated
6 tablespoons (90ml) cooked rice
1 tablespoon (15ml) parsley, chopped
1 teaspoon (5ml) Marmite
1 tablespoon (15ml) soy sauce
2 eggs, beaten
4 tablespoons (60ml) cheese, grated

Pre-heat oven to 190°C/375°F/Gas 5. Fry onion and garlic in oil until soft. Add lentils and stock and cook until stock is absorbed. Remove from heat and add all other ingredients, mixing well. Put into a 11 x 7 in (28 x 18 cm) baking tin which has been greased and lined with baking paper. Cook in pre-heated oven for 45-50 minutes until brown and firm to the touch. Serve with new potatoes and chutneys.

Sesame and Nut Roast
Serves 2

1 onion, finely chopped
1 tablespoon (15ml) olive oil
stock made with 1 teaspoon (5ml) vegetable extract, dissolved in 4 fl oz (100ml) hot water
4 oz (100g) Brazil nuts, chopped or grated
2 oz (50g) sesame seeds
2 slices wholemeal bread, crumbled
1 tablespoon (15ml) wholemeal flour
pinch of mixed herbs

Pre-heat oven to 190°C/375°F/Gas 5. Fry the onion in oil until soft, then add stock. Line a small casserole dish with greased foil. Mix all ingredients together and press into the dish. Bake in pre-heated oven for 30-40 minutes until firm to the touch. Serve with boiled potatoes and tomato ketchup.

Nut Roast
Serves 2

> 1 onion, chopped
> 1 clove garlic, crushed
> knob of butter
> 4 oz (100g) chopped mixed nuts
> 2 oz (50g) soft wholemeal breadcrumbs
> 1 teaspoon (5ml) Marmite
> 1 carrot, grated
> 1 egg, beaten
> sprinkling of mixed herbs
> salt and pepper

Pre-heat oven to 190°C/375°F/Gas 5. Fry onion and garlic in butter until browning. Mix with the rest of ingredients. Put into a greased loaf tin, and press down well. Bake in pre-heated oven for 30 minutes. Serve with chutney and salad.

Stuffed Nut Roast
Serves 4-6

This is my all-time favourite vegetarian dish, and I have used it on many occasions when entertaining. However, because it is tasty whether served hot or cold, it is also a good dish to make at the weekend, leaving some to be served cold during the week.

Nutmeat:
4 oz (100g) pine nuts
2 oz (50g) cashews
2 oz (50g) almonds
1 onion, chopped
1 oz (25g) butter
4 tablespoons (60ml) milk
2 eggs, beaten
4 oz (100g) wholemeal breadcrumbs
salt and pepper
pinch of nutmeg

Stuffing:
1 sachet vegetarian stuffing
4 oz (100g) mushrooms, chopped
1 oz (25g) butter
1 clove garlic, crushed
soy sauce
pinch of mixed herbs

Pre-heat oven to 200°C/400°F/Gas 6. Grind the pine nuts, cashews and almonds. Fry onion in butter until soft. Mix together all nutmeat ingredients. Make up the stuffing as directed on the packet. Then cook the mushrooms in the butter for a few minutes with garlic. Add to the stuffing and season with soy sauce and herbs. Grease a 1 lb loaf tin very well. Put half the nutmeat into the tin and press down well. Cover with all the stuffing and top with the rest of the nutmeat. Cover with foil, and cook in pre-heated oven for 1 hour. To brown the top, remove the foil, and cook for a further 10 minutes. Cool in the tin for 5 minutes before turning out. Serve hot with onion gravy (see p. 161), or cold with chutneys.

Courgette and Nut Roast
Serves 4

> 8 oz (200g) mixed nuts, toasted and finely chopped
> 1 lb (400g) courgettes, grated
> 4 oz (100g) fresh wholemeal breadcrumbs
> 1 red pepper, finely chopped
> 1 tablespoon (15ml) oil
> 1 onion, finely chopped
> 1 tablespoon (15ml) pesto
> 2 eggs, beaten

Pre-heat oven to 190°C/375°F/Gas 5. Mix all ingredients together and place in a well-greased ovenproof dish. Cook in pre-heated oven for 40 minutes, until firm to the touch and brown on top. Remove from oven and let rest for 5 minutes. Cut into squares. Serve hot or cold. This is particularly good with tomato sauce (see p. 139), new potatoes and a green vegetable or salad.

Stuffed Courgettes
Serves 2

> 4 courgettes
> 2 tomatoes, chopped
> 1 tablespoon (15ml) olive oil
> 2 teaspoons (10ml) tomato purée
> 2 tablespoons (30ml) hazelnuts, chopped
> sprinkling of Italian seasoning
> sprinkling of Tabasco sauce

Pre-heat oven to 190°C/375°F/Gas 5. Cut one side off each courgette. On opposite side of each, cut a sliver of skin off to allow courgette to sit flat on the plate. Working on the cut-off side of each courgette, scoop out inside flesh, leaving ends and a thickish shell – so you have a boat shape. Finely chop flesh and fry with tomatoes in oil until soft. Mix in the other ingredients and use this mixture to stuff courgettes. Place courgettes on a baking tray and cook in pre-heated oven for 25 minutes. Serve with chips or new potatoes and peas.

Stuffed Aubergine
Serves 2

1 large aubergine, halved lengthways
1 onion, chopped
1 clove garlic, crushed
2 tablespoons (30ml) olive oil
2 oz (50g) mushrooms, chopped
7-oz (200-g) can chopped tomatoes
1 tablespoon (15ml) tomato purée
sprinkling of Italian herbs
1 tablespoon (15ml) parsley, chopped
2 tablespoons (30ml) fresh breadcrumbs
1 tablespoon (15ml) chopped mixed nuts

Pre-heat oven to 200°C/400°F/Gas 6. Scoop out the aubergine flesh from both halves, leaving two shells. Place shells in shallow ovenproof dish. Chop flesh and fry gently with onion and garlic in oil for 10 minutes. Add mushrooms and fry for a further minute before mixing in tomatoes, tomato purée and herbs. Use this mixture to stuff shells. Dry-fry breadcrumbs and nuts for a few minutes until brown and then sprinkle over aubergine. Bake in pre-heated oven for 25 minutes. Serve with garlic bread and salad.

Apple and Stilton-stuffed Jackets
Serves 2

> 2 x 6-8 oz (2 x 150-200g) baking potatoes
> oil
> 1 apple, cored and cubed
> 4 oz (100g) Stilton, crumbled
> 1 tablespoon (15ml) soft margarine or butter
> 1 tablespoon (15ml) mayonnaise
> salt and pepper

Pre-heat oven to 200°C/400°F/Gas 6. Brush potatoes with oil and bake in pre-heated oven for 75 minutes. Cut in half lengthways and scoop out potato flesh. Mash with other ingredients and pile back into the potato jackets. Rough up surface of potato mixture and grill under a hot grill until it starts to brown. Serve with salad and garlic bread.

Marmite and Cheese-stuffed Jackets
Serves 2

> 2 x 6-8 oz (2 x 150-200g) baking potatoes
> oil
> 2 oz (50g) cheese, grated
> 1 tablespoon (15ml) soft margarine or butter
> Marmite

Pre-heat oven to 200°C/400°F/Gas 6. Brush potatoes with oil and bake in pre-heated oven for 75 minutes. Cut in half lengthways and scoop out potato flesh. Mash this together with cheese and margarine or butter. Add Marmite to taste. Pile mixture back into potato jackets, and rough up surface with a fork. Cook under a hot grill until potato surface starts to brown. Serve with salad.

Mushroom-stuffed Jackets
Serves 2

> 2 x 6-8 oz (2 x 150-200g) baking potatoes
> oil
> 4 oz (100g) mushrooms, chopped
> few spring onions, finely chopped
> 1 clove garlic, crushed
> 1 tablespoon (15ml) margarine

Pre-heat oven to 200°C/400°F/Gas 6. Rub potatoes with oil and cook in pre-heated oven for 75 minutes. Fry the mushrooms, onions and garlic in margarine for 5 minutes. When potatoes are cooked, cut in half lengthways and scoop out flesh, then mix with mushroom mixture and pile back into potato skins. Grill under a hot grill until brown. Serve with salad and garlic bread.

Pepper-stuffed Courgettes
Serves 2

2 large courgettes
1 red pepper, diced
1 clove garlic, crushed
2 tablespoons (30ml) oil
2 tablespoons (30ml) canned chopped tomatoes
2 tablespoons (30ml) red pesto
2 tablespoons (30ml) fresh breadcrumbs
2 tablespoons (30ml) cheese, grated

Cook courgettes in boiling water for 5 minutes, drain and cut off ends. Halve each lengthways and scoop out the middles, leaving a shell which you can stuff. Fry pepper and garlic in 1 tablespoon (15ml) of oil until soft. Mix with tomatoes and pesto, and use to stuff courgette shells. Stir-fry breadcrumbs in remaining oil until crisp. Mix with cheese and use to top courgettes. Put courgettes in an ovenproof dish and grill until top is browning. Serve with salad.

Nut-stuffed Peppers
Serves 2

2 red peppers
1 onion, chopped
1 clove garlic, crushed
2 tablespoons (30ml) oil
2 oz (50g) nuts, chopped
1 tablespoon (15ml) tomato purée
2 tablespoons (30ml) canned chopped tomatoes
4 oz (100g) cooked rice
1 tablespoon (15ml) parsley, chopped
salt and pepper
2 tablespoons (30ml) cheese, grated

Pre-heat oven to 180°C/350°F/Gas 4. Cut peppers in half and take out seeds. Cook in boiling water for 5 minutes. Drain. Fry onion and garlic in oil until soft. Add all other ingredients except cheese and heat through. Lay peppers in a heatproof dish and fill with stuffing (any extra can be put around the peppers). Sprinkle with cheese and bake in pre-heated oven for 25-30 minutes until cheese has melted. Serve with salad.

Baked Stuffed Avocados
Serves 2

1 onion, diced
1 clove garlic, crushed
1 tablespoon (15ml) oil
4 oz (100g) mushrooms, diced
knob of butter
2 tablespoons (30ml) nuts, chopped
1 teaspoon (5ml) soy sauce
1 teaspoon (5ml) tomato purée
sprinkling of Tabasco sauce
1 large or 2 small avocados
2 tablespoons (30ml) cheese, grated

Pre-heat oven to 200°C/400°F/Gas 6. Fry the onion and garlic in oil until soft. Add mushrooms and butter and cook for a further 5 minutes. Add nuts, soy sauce, tomato purée and Tabasco. Mix well. Cut avocados in half and remove stone. Place in an ovenproof dish and stuff with mixture. Extra stuffing can be placed around avocado. Sprinkle with cheese and bake in pre-heated oven for 20 minutes. Serve with salad.

Spicy Stuffed Tomatoes
Serves 2

1 onion, chopped
1 clove garlic, crushed
1 teaspoon (5ml) 'lazy' chilli
1 tablespoon (15ml) oil
2 beefsteak tomatoes
1 tablespoon (15ml) tomato purée
2 tablespoons (30ml) canned sweetcorn
2 tablespoons (30ml) cooked rice
sprinkling of Tabasco sauce
2 tablespoons (30ml) cheese, grated

Pre-heat oven to 200°C/400°F/Gas 6. Fry onion, garlic and the chilli in oil until soft. Cut tops off tomatoes and scoop out the insides. Mix the tomato flesh with all other ingredients except cheese. Refill tomatoes and place in an ovenproof dish. Sprinkle with cheese and bake in pre-heated oven for 15-20 minutes until cheese melts. Serve with salad and garlic bread.

Pancakes
Makes 6-8

    batter (see p. 164)
batter (see p. 164)
    oil for cooking

Heat a little oil in a frying pan and add enough batter to cover the bottom of the pan. Fry until bottom has started to brown (lift pancake at edge to check). Flip(!) the pancake over and cook for a further minute or two, to brown other side. Keep warm whilst making rest of pancakes.

Pancake fillings

A number of different styles of pancakes can be made by varying the fillings. Just mix the different ingredients together and use to stuff the pancakes before folding and serving.

ITALIAN STYLE
Curd cheese, a pinch of basil and chopped spring onion.

CHINESE STYLE
Fry some beansprouts in groundnut oil, add soy sauce, sliced mushrooms and grated fresh ginger.

FRENCH STYLE
Fry chopped mushrooms with garlic, and add a little cream.

SWISS STYLE
Mix grated Gruyère cheese with cream and season with black pepper.

Bean-stuffed Pancakes
Serves 2

4 pancakes (see p. 97 and p. 164)
1 onion, chopped
1 clove garlic, crushed
1 tablespoon (15ml) oil
2 tablespoons (30ml) canned chopped tomatoes
2 tablespoons (30ml) canned red kidney beans
4 oz (100g) spinach, chopped
1 teaspoon (5ml) sugar
1 tablespoon (15ml) tomato purée
2 oz (50g) cheese, grated

Keep pancakes warm whilst making stuffing. Fry onion and garlic in oil until soft. Add all other ingredients except cheese and cook on a gentle heat for 4-5 minutes until spinach has cooked. Divide mixture between pancakes and fold up, put in heatproof dish and cover with cheese. Grill until cheese melts. This is very good served with salsa sauce (see p. 170) and salad.

Cheese 'n' Veg-stuffed Pancakes
Serves 2

4 pancakes (see p. 97 and p. 164)
1 pepper, diced
1 carrot, diced
3 tablespoons (45ml) oil
1 courgette, sliced
few spring onions, chopped
2 tablespoons (30ml) Greek yoghurt
4 oz (100g) cheese, grated

Keep pancakes warm whilst making stuffing. Cook pepper and carrot in oil until soft. Add courgette and onions and cook for a further 2 minutes. Add yoghurt and half of cheese and warm through. Use this mixture to stuff pancakes. Fold pancakes up and put in a heatproof dish, sprinkle with remaining cheese and grill until cheese melts. Serve with salad.

Burritos (Stuffed Tortillas)
Serves 2

    4 flour tortillas
    refried beans (see p. 169)
    2 tablespoons (30ml) canned chopped tomatoes
    2 oz (50g) cheese, grated

Pre-heat oven to 180°C/350°F/Gas 4. In the middle of each tortilla place a tablespoon of refried beans. Top with tomatoes and cheese, fold each tortilla into a parcel and place in an ovenproof dish. Cook in pre-heated oven for 20 minutes. Serve with guacamole, salsa sauce (see p. 169 and p. 170), and sour cream.

6 Quick Fries

Whenever you are in a hurry to eat, there is no doubt that the quickest way to produce a meal is to reach for the frying pan or wok and do a quick fry. There is no need to worry about these being unhealthy, as long as you are careful about what oil you use and the quantities that you are using. Also, you tend not to use so much cheese in your cooking when frying, so this keeps the level of saturated fats that you are using down.

Most vegetables can be fried, and with different combinations of beans, nuts and seasonings many interesting and tasty dishes can be concocted quickly. I have given some of our favourites here – so get out that trusty frying pan or wok and try out some of these ideas. Hopefully, they will inspire you to try out some recipe ideas of your own.

Spicy Piperade
Serves 2

> 2 tablespoons (30ml) olive oil
> 1 onion, sliced
> 2 cloves garlic, chopped or crushed
> 1 red pepper, sliced
> 7-oz (200-g) can chopped tomatoes
> 1 teaspoon (5ml) chilli sauce or paste
> 1 teaspoon (5ml) pesto
> 2 teaspoons (10ml) tomato purée
> 3 eggs, beaten

Heat the oil and gently fry the onion, garlic and pepper until soft. Add all other ingredients except eggs and leave to simmer gently for 5 minutes, until sauce has reduced and thickened. Add eggs and, stirring continuously, cook until eggs are creamy and barely set. Serve immediately with garlic bread.

Garlicky Buttered Lentils
Serves 2

> 1 onion, chopped
> 2 cloves garlic, crushed
> 2 tablespoons (30ml) oil
> 6 oz (150g) green lentils
> 7-oz (200-g) can chopped tomatoes
> 10 fl oz (250ml) stock
> 2 oz (50g) garlic butter
> 1 tablespoon (15ml) parsley, chopped

Fry onion and garlic in oil until soft. Add lentils, tomatoes and stock. Bring to boil, cover and simmer for 25 minutes. Stir in garlic butter and parsley. Serve with French bread and salad.

Vegetable Goulash
Serves 2

> 1 onion, chopped
> 1 teaspoon (5ml) garlic purée
> 2 tablespoons (30ml) oil
> 8 oz (200g) potatoes, cubed
> 8 oz (200g) carrots, cubed
> 8 oz (200g) courgettes, sliced
> 1 red pepper, cubed
> 14-oz (400-g) can chopped tomatoes
> 1 tablespoon (15ml) tomato purée
> 1 tablespoon (15ml) paprika

Fry onion and garlic purée in oil until soft. Add rest of ingredients and bring to boil. Reduce heat and simmer until vegetables are cooked through (approximately 30 minutes). Serve with buttered noodles or brown rice.

Vegetable Stir-fry
Serves 2

> 1 tablespoon (15ml) oil
> 1 red pepper, cut into strips
> 1 green pepper, cut into strips
> 1 courgette, cut into rounds
> 4 oz (100g) mushrooms, sliced
> 1 teaspoon (5ml) garlic purée
> 1 teaspoon (5ml) ginger purée
> 1 tablespoon (15ml) soy sauce
> 2 tablespoons (30ml) sherry or orange juice

Heat the oil in your wok or a large frying pan. Add all of the vegetables with the garlic and ginger purées, and quickly stir-fry for 2 minutes. Add the soy sauce and sherry or orange juice and fry for a further minute. Serve immediately with rice or noodles.

Cheesy Eggs and Veg
Serves 2

> knob of butter
> 6 eggs, beaten
> salt and pepper
> 8 oz (200g) cooked vegetables – I suggest corn,
>   chopped broccoli or even asparagus, if you're
>   feeling rich
> 2 oz (50g) Cheddar cheese, grated

Melt half of butter in a frying pan and add eggs. Whilst frying
them, keep stirring with a wooden spoon or a fork. Season.
When eggs are starting to set, add vegetables and rest of
butter. Cover with cheese and continue cooking until the
cheese melts. Serve with new potatoes or hot buttered toast.
A tomato side salad goes well with this – or even just tomato
ketchup.

Quick Sweet 'n' Sour
Serves 2

> 1 carrot, diced
> 1 pepper, diced
> small bunch of spring onions, chopped
> 2 tablespoons (30ml) groundnut oil
> 3 tablespoons (45ml) juice from canned pineapple
> 3 tablespoons (45ml) tomato ketchup
> 2 tablespoons (30ml) soy sauce
> 1 tablespoon (15ml) wine vinegar
> 2 teaspoons (10ml) cornflour
> 8 oz (200g) fresh beansprouts
> 8-oz (200-g) can pineapple chunks
> 8-oz (200-g) can bamboo shoots

Fry the carrot, pepper and onions in oil for 4 minutes. Mix
together the pineapple juice, tomato ketchup, soy sauce,
wine vinegar and cornflour. Add to the vegetables and bring
to the boil. Simmer for 2 minutes. Add rest of ingredients and
stir-fry for 2 minutes. Serve immediately with rice or noodles.

Indonesian Beans and Carrots
Serves 2

1 teaspoon (5ml) 'lazy' chilli
1 teaspoon (5ml) 'lazy' ginger
1 clove garlic, crushed
pinch of curry powder or paste
2 tablespoons (30ml) groundnut oil
8 oz (200g) green beans, sliced
1 large carrot, cut into matchsticks
5 fl oz (125ml) water
1 tablespoon (15ml) crunchy peanut butter
squeeze of lime juice

Fry the chilli, ginger, garlic and curry powder in oil for 1 minute. Add beans and carrot and stir-fry for 2 minutes. Add the water, bring to the boil and simmer until only a little water is left. Stir in the peanut butter. Mix well, and stir in lime juice. Serve with noodles or rice.

Peanut, Broccoli and Corn Stir-fry
Serves 2

small bunch of spring onions, chopped
1 clove garlic, crushed
2 tablespoons (30ml) groundnut oil
8 oz (200g) broccoli florets, diced
1 carrot, grated
8-oz (200-g) can sweetcorn, drained
2 tablespoons (30ml) crunchy peanut butter
2 tablespoons (30ml) soy sauce
sprinkling of Tabasco sauce

Fry onions and garlic in oil for 2 minutes. Add other vegetables and cook for 3 minutes. Stir in peanut butter and soy sauce, and sprinkle with Tabasco. Serve with noodles or rice.

Cheesy Butter Beans
Serves 2

> 1 onion, chopped
> 1 tablespoon (15ml) oil
> 5 fl oz (125ml) Greek yoghurt
> 16-oz (400-g) can butter beans, drained
> 4 oz (100g) cheese, grated
> black pepper

Fry onion in oil until brown, then turn heat down and add yoghurt and butter beans. Add cheese and continue to cook until cheese has melted. Season and serve with jacket or new potatoes and a side salad.

Spiced Chickpeas
Serves 2

> 1 onion, chopped
> 1 clove garlic, crushed
> 1 tablespoon (15ml) groundnut oil
> 2 teaspoons (10ml) curry powder or paste
> 2 tablespoons (30ml) Greek yoghurt
> 1 teaspoon (5ml) tomato purée
> 16-oz (400-g) can chickpeas, drained

Fry onion and garlic in oil until brown. Add curry powder and stir-fry for 1 minute. Add rest of ingredients and continue stir-frying until heated through. Serve with rice.

Broccoli with Noodles
Serves 2

    4 oz (100g) noodles
    1 clove garlic, crushed
    1 tablespoon (15ml) groundnut oil
    12 oz (300g) broccoli florets, diced
    5 fl oz (125ml) water
    salt and pepper
    knob of butter
    sprinkling of Parmesan cheese (optional)

Put noodles into boiling water to cook. Meanwhile, fry garlic in oil for 1 minute. Add broccoli and fry for 3 minutes. Add water and simmer gently for 5 minutes – the broccoli will absorb the water. Season and stir in the butter. Mix into the noodles, adding the Parmesan cheese if you like. Serve with a mixed salad.

Vegetable Chow Mein
Serves 2

    1 onion, finely sliced
    2 tablespoons (30ml) groundnut oil
    2 sticks celery, finely sliced
    4 oz (100g) mushrooms, sliced
    1 pepper, diced
    1 tablespoon (15ml) soy sauce
    1 tablespoon (15ml) sherry or dry Martini
    1 teaspoon (5ml) sugar
    1 teaspoon (5ml) wine vinegar
    4 oz (100g) noodles, cooked
    4 oz (100g) fresh beansprouts

Fry the onion in the oil until starting to colour. Add the rest of vegetables and continue to stir-fry for 3 minutes. Add soy sauce, sherry, sugar and wine vinegar and cook for another minute. Finally, stir in noodles and beansprouts and stir-fry for 2 minutes. Serve immediately.

Creamed Mushrooms
Serves 2

> 1 onion, chopped
> 1 green pepper (optional)
> 2 tablespoons (30ml) groundnut oil
> 8 oz (200g) mushrooms, sliced
> large knob of butter
> 5 fl oz (125ml) single cream
> black pepper

Fry the onion, and pepper if using, in oil until soft. You will need 2 tablespoons oil if using both onion and pepper. Add the mushrooms and butter and cook until juices flow. Add the cream and simmer gently until heated through. Season and serve with jacket or new potatoes and a green vegetable.

Sweet Peanut Fry
Serves 2

This may sound rather odd, but I assure you that it is absolutely delicious.

> small bunch of spring onions, chopped
> 1 clove garlic, crushed
> 2 medium carrots, grated
> 1 red pepper, chopped
> 2 tablespoons (30ml) groundnut oil
> 2 tablespoons (30ml) crunchy peanut butter
> 2 tablespoons (30ml) soy sauce
> 2 tablespoons (30ml) honey
> 2 oz (50g) unsalted peanuts
> 8 oz (200g) fresh beansprouts

Fry onions, garlic, carrots, and pepper in oil until starting to brown. Add peanut butter, soy sauce and honey and stir-fry for 1 minute. Add peanuts and beansprouts and stir-fry for 2 minutes. Serve with noodles or rice.

Coconut and Cashew Stir-fry
Serves 2

    8 oz (200g) white cabbage, finely shredded
    2 carrots, grated
    2 tablespoons (30ml) groundnut oil
    2 teaspoons (10ml) curry powder or paste
    5 fl oz (125ml) Greek yoghurt
    2 oz (50g) cashews
    4 tablespoons (60ml) grated or desiccated coconut

Stir-fry cabbage and carrots in oil for 3 minutes. Add curry powder and stir-fry for 1 minute. Add yoghurt, cashews and coconut and stir-fry until heated throughout. Serve with rice.

Herby Fries
Serves 2

    4 slices bread, crumbed
    2 oz (50g) mixed chopped nuts
    small onion, finely chopped
    4 tablespoons (60ml) fresh herbs
    3 eggs, beaten
    salt and pepper
    oil, for frying

Bind together the breadcrumbs, nuts, onion, herbs and eggs. Season. Heat some oil in a frying pan, using enough to cover the base. Place small mounds of the herb mixture in the pan and fry for 2-3 minutes on each side until crisp. Serve with tomato relish or ketchup and a green vegetable, or with baked beans and grilled tomatoes.

Nut Fritters
Serves 2

> 2 tablespoons (30ml) self-raising wholemeal flour
> 1 egg, beaten
> 4 tablespoons (60ml) milk
> 2 oz (50g) chopped nuts
> 2 tablespoons (30ml) fresh breadcrumbs
> 1 clove garlic, crushed
> small bunch of spring onions, chopped
> salt and pepper
> oil, for frying

Mix the flour, egg and milk together to make a batter. Add rest of ingredients, except for oil, and mix. In a frying pan, heat enough oil to cover the base. When hot, put tablespoons of the mixture in. Cook for a few minutes on either side until brown. Serve with new potatoes and salad.

Bean Burgers
Serves 2

> 8-oz (200-g) can butter beans, drained
> 2 oz (50g) fresh breadcrumbs or cooked rice
> 1 oz (25g) chopped mixed nuts
> 2 oz (50g) Cheddar cheese, grated
> 1 clove garlic, crushed
> 1 oz (25g) onion, finely chopped
> sprinkling of mixed herbs
> salt and pepper
> 1 egg white, beaten
> dried breadcrumbs
> oil, for frying

Mash the beans and mix with the breadcrumbs or rice, nuts, cheese, garlic and onion. Season with herbs, salt and pepper. Shape into 'burger' shapes. Dip into egg white and then coat with dried breadcrumbs. Heat enough oil in a frying pan to cover the base. Cook for 4 minutes on each side. Serve with baps and salad.

Veggie Burgers
Serves 2

    1 onion, finely chopped
    1 clove garlic, crushed
    4 oz (100g) mushrooms, finely chopped
    2 oz (50g) chopped mixed nuts
    2 oz (50g) fresh breadcrumbs
    1 tablespoon (15ml) wholemeal flour
    1 egg, beaten
    salt and pepper
    dried breadcrumbs
    oil, for frying

Mix together all ingredients except dried breadcrumbs and oil. Shape mixture into 'burger' shapes. Coat with dried breadcrumbs. Heat enough oil in a frying pan to cover the base. Cook the burgers for 4 minutes on each side. Serve with baps and salad.

Glamorgan Sausages
Serves 2

    4 oz (100g) fresh breadcrumbs
    4 oz (100g) Cheddar cheese, grated
    1 oz (25g) onion, finely chopped
    pinch of mustard powder
    salt and pepper
    sprinkling of herbs
    1 egg, separated
    dried breadcrumbs
    oil, for frying

Mix together the fresh breadcrumbs, cheese and onion. Season with mustard powder, salt and pepper, and herbs. Use the egg yolk, beaten, to bind the mixture together. Add a little water if it needs any more moisture, but the mixture should be quite firm. Form into 'sausage' shapes. Beat the egg white and dip the 'sausages' into it, then into dried bread-crumbs. Heat enough oil in a frying pan to cover the base. Cook the sausages on all sides until brown and crisp, which should take about 8 minutes. Good with chips and baked beans or salad and chutneys.

Peppery Potato Fry
Serves 2

2 peppers of different colours, diced
1 small onion, finely chopped
1 clove garlic, crushed
2 tablespoons (30ml) olive oil
10 oz (250g) cooked potatoes, diced
sprinkling of Tabasco sauce
salt and pepper
5 fl oz (125ml) vegetable stock

Cook peppers, onion and garlic in oil until soft. Add potatoes and continue cooking until browning at edges. Season to taste with Tabasco, salt and pepper. Pour stock over and flatten into 'cake'. Turn heat down and cook until stock is absorbed. Serve with salad.

Spinach and Bean Stir-fry
Serves 2

small bunch of spring onions, chopped
1 clove garlic, crushed
1 teaspoon (5ml) 'lazy' ginger
2 tablespoons (30ml) groundnut oil
4 oz (100g) spinach, cut into strips
4 oz (100g) green beans, sliced
5 fl oz (125ml) vegetable stock
2 tablespoons (30ml) sherry or apple juice
2 tablespoons (30ml) soy sauce
1 teaspoon (5ml) cornflour
8 oz (200g) fresh beansprouts

Stir-fry the spring onions, garlic and ginger in oil for 1 minute. Add the spinach and green beans. Continue to stir-fry for a further minute. Mix stock, sherry, soy sauce and cornflour together. Add to vegetables. When bubbling, add bean-sprouts and cook for 2 minutes. Serve with rice or noodles.

Bean Amandine
Serves 2

1 onion, finely chopped
1 clove garlic, crushed
large knob of butter
12 oz (300g) French beans, sliced
1 teaspoon (5ml) paprika
5 fl oz (125ml) vegetable stock
5 fl oz (125ml) sour cream
2 oz (50g) toasted flaked almonds

Fry the onion and garlic in butter until soft. Add beans, paprika and stock. Bring to the boil, cover and simmer for 6 minutes. Stir the sour cream and almonds into the dish and gently heat through. Serve with rice or noodles and garnish with more paprika.

Spanish Omelette
Serves 2

1 onion, finely chopped
1 clove garlic, crushed
1 pepper, diced
3 tablespoons (45ml) olive oil
12 oz (300g) cooked potatoes, diced
4 eggs, beaten
salt and pepper
sprinkling of oregano

Cook onion, garlic and pepper in oil for 5 minutes. Add potatoes and continue cooking until potato is browning at edges. Beat eggs together with salt and pepper and oregano and pour into pan with vegetables. Stir well. Continue to cook for a few minutes until egg is setting. Finish off under a hot grill to brown top. Serve with salad.

Creamed Leeks with Walnuts
Serves 2

16 oz (400g) leeks, chopped
large knob of butter
5 fl oz (125ml) vegetable stock
1 tablespoon (15ml) chopped parsley
1 tablespoon (15ml) creamed horseradish
5 fl oz (125ml) whipping cream
2 teaspoons (10ml) cornflour
salt and pepper
4 oz (100g) shelled walnuts, halved

Fry leeks in butter until soft – about 3 minutes. Add the stock, parsley and horseradish and bring to the boil. Cover and simmer gently for 5 minutes. Blend the whipping cream and cornflour together. Season and add to sauce with walnuts. Cook for a few minutes until sauce thickens. Serve with rice or baked potatoes.

Speedy Ratatouille
Serves 2

> 1 small aubergine, diced
> 1 courgette, sliced
> 1 red pepper, diced
> 2 cloves garlic, crushed
> 3 tablespoons (45ml) olive oil
> 14-oz (400-g) can chopped tomatoes
> sprinkling of mixed herbs
> salt and pepper
> splash of red wine
> olive oil (optional)

Fry aubergine, courgette, pepper and garlic in oil until soft — about 5 minutes. Add tomatoes, herbs and seasoning. Cover and simmer for 15 minutes. Just before serving, I add a splash of red wine and some more olive oil. Serve with brown rice or crusty bread.

Beer Fondue
Serves 2

> 10 fl oz (250ml) beer
> 10 oz (250g) cheese, grated
> 1 clove garlic, crushed
> 1 tablespoon (15ml) cornflour, mixed with a little cold
>   water
> 1 oz (25g) butter (optional)
> 1 teaspoon (5ml) French mustard

Place beer, cheese and garlic in saucepan. Heat gently until cheese melts. Add cornflour mixture, butter (if used) and mustard. Keep stirring while mixture thickens and bubbles. Serve with French bread, which should be dipped into the fondue.

Broccoli and Pepper Stir-fry
Serves 2

> 1 onion, chopped
> 1 red pepper, sliced
> 1 green pepper, sliced
> 1 tablespoon (15ml) oil
> 4 oz (100g) broccoli, diced
> 3 tablespoons (45ml) hot vegetable stock
> 2 tablespoons (30ml) black bean sauce
> 1 tablespoon (15ml) runny honey

Stir-fry the onion and peppers in the oil for 3 minutes. Add the broccoli and continue to fry for a further 2 minutes. Add the stock, black bean sauce and honey. Cook for a further minute. Serve with rice.

Oriental Vegetables
Serves 2

1 small aubergine, diced
4 tablespoons (60ml) oil
small bunch of spring onions, chopped
2 oz (50g) mushrooms, sliced
8-oz (200-g) can water chestnuts, drained and sliced
2 oz (50g) spinach leaves, shredded
2 tablespoons (30ml) oyster or soy sauce
sprinkling of sesame seeds

Fry the aubergine in 2 tablespoons oil for 5 minutes, until starting to brown. Adding onions, mushrooms, water chestnuts and rest of oil, stir-fry for 2 minutes. Add spinach and oyster or soy sauce. Cook for a further minute. Garnish with sesame seeds before serving with rice.

Cheese and Herb Risotto
Serves 2

1 onion, finely chopped
1 clove garlic, crushed
2 tablespoons (30ml) oil
4 oz (100g) long grain rice
10 fl oz (250g) vegetable stock
14-oz (400-g) can chopped tomatoes
4 oz (100g) Cheddar cheese, grated
1 tablespoon (15ml) chives, chopped
1 tablespoon (15ml) parsley, chopped

Fry the onion and garlic in oil until soft. Add the rice and fry for 2 minutes. Add the stock and tomatoes. Bring to the boil and then cover and simmer until rice is cooked and most of the liquid is absorbed (approximately 15-20 minutes). Stir in half of cheese and all the herbs. Serve sprinkled with rest of cheese. This is very good with garlic bread and a green salad.

Basic Omelette
Serves 1

> 2-3 eggs (depending on appetite)
> 1 tablespoon (15ml) cold water
> salt and pepper
> knob of butter

Beat the eggs and then add water and season to taste. Heat a frying (or omelette) pan. When hot, add the butter and swirl it round, letting it melt. Quickly add the egg mixture and, with a wooden spoon, keep drawing the egg into the middle, letting the uncooked egg run to the sides of the pan. When the egg has set, leave to cook for 1 minute. A perfect omelette will be golden underneath and still a little creamy on top. Serve plain or place chosen filling in middle of omelette and slide onto your plate, folding one side over the other as you do so. Some people prefer to fold both sides on top of each other and then tip omelette out with folds underneath — do whatever you think is easiest. Serve with peas and sweetcorn.

A number of different omelettes can be made by varying the fillings. Just place in the middle of the omelette before folding and serving.

MUSHROOM
Fry 2 oz (50g) diced mushrooms in a knob of butter until soft.

TOMATO
Fry 2 chopped tomatoes, and 1 teaspoon (5ml) of tomato purée, in a knob of butter for 2 minutes.

SWEETCORN
Just add 2 tablespoons (30ml) of canned sweetcorn kernels.

BROCCOLI
Fry 2 oz (50g) of diced broccoli in a knob of butter for 2 minutes.

CHEESE
Add 3 tablespoons (15ml) of grated cheese to the middle of the omelette.

Peppery Omelette
Serves 2

> 2 small peppers of different colours, chopped
> 1 clove garlic, crushed
> 2 tablespoons (30ml) oil
> 4 eggs, beaten
> 2 oz (30g) cheese, grated
> sprinkling of Tabasco sauce
> salt and pepper

Fry pepper and garlic in oil until soft. Add eggs and cheese and seasonings. Draw the egg into the middle of the pan, letting the uncooked egg run to the side of the pan. Then let cook for 1-2 minutes. Finish under grill to brown.

Bean Omelette
Serves 2

> 1 onion, chopped
> 1 red pepper, diced
> 2 tablespoons (30ml) oil
> 8-oz (200-g) can kidney beans, drained
> 4 eggs, beaten

Fry the onion and pepper in oil until soft. Add beans and then eggs. With a wooden spoon, keep drawing the eggs into the middle of the pan, letting the uncooked egg run to the side of the pan. When egg has set, leave to cook for 1 minute. Finish under a hot grill to brown top.

Apple and Vegetable Stir-fry
Serves 2

1 onion, sliced
1 red pepper, sliced
2 courgettes, sliced
sprinkling of basil
2 dessert apples, sliced
3 tablespoons oil
1 teaspoon (5ml) brown sugar
1 teaspoon (5ml) vinegar
14-oz (400-g) can chopped tomatoes
1 tablespoon (15ml) tomato purée

Fry onion, pepper, courgettes, basil and apple in oil for 10 minutes. Add sugar and vinegar and stir-fry until sugar melts. Add rest of ingredients and simmer for 15 minutes. Serve with rice.

Chilli sin Carne
Serves 4

1 onion, chopped
1 clove garlic, crushed
1 green pepper, chopped
2 tablespoons (30ml) oil
10 oz (250g) minced Quorn
2 tablespoons (30ml) tomato purée
14-oz (400-g) can chopped tomatoes
1 packet Old El Paso chilli mix
16-oz (400-g) can red kidney beans, drained

Fry the onion, garlic and pepper in oil until soft. Add Quorn and continue to cook until brown. Add rest of ingredients and mix well. Cover tightly and simmer gently for 15 minutes. Serve with rice.

Vegetable Couscous
Serves 2

1 aubergine, diced
1 red pepper, diced
1 onion, chopped
1 teaspoon (5ml) garlic purée
1 teaspoon (5ml) ginger purée
1 teaspoon (5ml) coriander
1 teaspoon (5ml) cumin
pinch of cinnamon
4 tablespoons (60ml) oil
2 oz (50g) no-need-to-soak prunes, halved
2 oz (50g) no-need-to-soak apricots, halved
8 fl oz (200ml) vegetable stock
6 oz (150g) couscous

Fry vegetables, garlic, ginger and spices in oil. When onions are soft and beginning to colour, stir in the prunes, apricots and stock. Bring to the boil, cover and simmer gently for 5 minutes. Meanwhile, put the couscous in a bowl and cover with boiling water. Leave for 3 minutes. Drain and break up any lumps that have formed. Put in a metal colander (if the holes are rather large, put a piece of muslin or a new J-cloth in the bottom). Cover and steam over vegetables for 20 minutes. Serve the couscous with the vegetables and fruit spooned on top.

7 Pasta and Pizza

These forms of Italian cuisine are becoming ever more popular. There are innumerable types of both fresh and dried pasta available in the shops now. In many of these recipes I have not specified a particular type, so you can experiment with whatever types take your fancy – just be sure to cook them for the time specified on the packet. (If you transfer your pasta to an ornamental jar when you buy it, remember to make a note of how you should cook it!)

I have always been fond of pasta and I am glad to say that where once it was seen as a fattening food, this view has changed, and its nutritional value has now been recognised.

Many vegetarian cookery books specify wholemeal pasta in their recipes because of its fibre content. However, I do not agree with this view. I have to admit to having gone off wholemeal pasta – I much prefer the ordinary egg pasta, or spinach or tomato varieties, which I find much more tasty. And as the vegetarian diet contains much more fibre than the usual British diet, I feel that there is no need to stick to the wholemeal variety because it is 'healthier'. My advice is to choose the type you prefer – after all, it is you who will be eating it!

I must also admit that, since being given a pasta machine as a Christmas present (it's funny how many of my presents are connected with food), I have become a fresh pasta addict. These machines really are very simple, and fun, to use, so I can recommend them most heartily. However, dried pasta is a very useful standby and of course comes in a great many varieties, so it still has a place in my cooking.

At the end of the pizza section is a recipe for calzoni – a stuffed pizza. If you have not tried these, they are great, especially as a filling lunch or late supper. The recipe I give can easily be adapted to your own favourite ingredients.

With pasta and pizza dishes, I tend to serve salad and sometimes also garlic bread – it depends on how naughty we are feeling!

I would only advise you to attempt making pasta if you are the proud owner of both a food processor and a pasta machine — then it really is simplicity itself!

Pasta Dough

4 oz (100g) plain flour
pinch of salt
1 egg, beaten

Put all ingredients into a food processor and whizz together to make a dough. If the dough seems sticky just add a little more flour. Cover and leave to stand in the refrigerator for 30 minutes before using. Follow the instructions for your pasta machine.

Tomato Pasta Dough

5 oz (125g) plain flour
pinch of salt
1 egg, beaten
1 tablespoon (15ml) tomato purée

Whizz all ingredients in a food processor to form a dough. Leave, covered, in the refrigerator for 30 minutes before shaping and using.

Lemon and Herb Pasta Dough

5 oz (125g) plain flour
pinch of salt
1 egg, beaten
squeeze of lemon (not too much!)
grated rind of half a lemon
sprinkling of mixed herbs

Place all ingredients in a food processor and whizz together until you have a dough. Leave, covered, for 30 minutes before shaping and using.

Mushroom Lasagne
Serves 4

    1 lb (400g) browncap mushrooms, chopped
    1 onion, chopped
    2 tablespoons (30ml) oil
    2 tablespoons (30ml) tomato purée
    1 teaspoon (5ml) mushroom ketchup
    glass of red wine
    14-oz (400-g) can chopped tomatoes
    15 fl oz (375ml) thick white sauce, made with 15 fl oz
      (375ml) milk (see p. 160)
    2 tablespoons (30ml) double cream
    6 oz (150g) lasagne
    8 oz (200g) cheese, grated

Pre-heat oven to 200°C/400°F/Gas 6. Fry mushrooms and onion in oil until soft. Add tomato purée, mushroom ketchup, red wine and tomatoes. Simmer for 10 minutes. Mix the white sauce and cream together. Alternately layer the mushroom sauce, lasagne, white sauce and cheese, ending with a layer of cheese. Bake in pre-heated oven for 40 minutes.

AUBERGINE LASAGNE

Follow the recipe above, but use 2 small or 1 large aubergine, diced, in place of the mushrooms.

Lentil and Carrot Lasagne
Serves 2

    1 onion, finely chopped
    1 teaspoon (5ml) garlic purée
    3 oz (75g) carrot, finely chopped
    1 tablespoon (15ml) oil
    3 oz (75g) green or brown lentils, cooked
    14-oz (400-g) can chopped tomatoes
    1 tablespoon (15ml) tomato purée
    1 tablespoon (15ml) fresh parsley, chopped
    salt and pepper
    3 oz (75g) lasagne
    6 oz (150g) cheese, grated

Pre-heat oven to 200°C/400°F/Gas 6. Fry onion, garlic purée and carrot in oil until soft. Mix with lentils, tomatoes, tomato purée and parsley. Season well. Put a layer of lasagne in a greased ovenproof dish, cover with half of lentil and carrot mixture, sprinkle with one-third of the cheese, add another layer of lasagne and the rest of the lentil and carrot mixture, and sprinkle with half of remaining cheese. Finally, put a last layer of lasagne on top and sprinkle with remaining cheese. Bake in pre-heated oven for 20 minutes. Serve with a green salad.

Spaghetti 'Bolognese'
Serves 2

This is the vegetarian version of spaghetti bolognese.

    1 onion, chopped
    1 clove garlic, crushed
    2 tablespoons (30ml) olive oil
    4 oz (100g) red split lentils
    7-oz (200-g) can chopped tomatoes
    1 tablespoon (15ml) tomato purée
    2 oz (50g) mushrooms, finely chopped
    6 oz (150g) spaghetti
    Parmesan, to serve

Fry onion and garlic in oil until soft. Add lentils and enough boiling water to cover. Cook for 10 minutes until water is absorbed. Add tomatoes, purée and mushrooms. Cover and simmer for 5 minutes. Meanwhile, cook spaghetti as directed on packet. When done, drain and mix with sauce. Serve with Parmesan cheese.

Pesto Pasta
Serves 2

    8 oz (200g) pasta quills (penne)
    knob of butter
    2 tablespoons (30ml) pesto
    sprinkling of Parmesan cheese

Cook pasta as packet directs. When *al dente*, drain and add butter. When butter has melted, add pesto and stir well. Place in bowls and sprinkle with Parmesan cheese. Serve with garlic bread.

Pasta with Mushrooms and Walnuts
Serves 2

6 oz (150g) pasta spirals or bows
1 onion, chopped
1 tablespoon (15ml) oil
knob of butter
4 oz (100g) mushrooms, sliced
2 oz (50g) walnuts, chopped
2 tablespoons (30ml) double cream
salt and pepper

Cook pasta as directed on packet. Whilst pasta is cooking, fry onion in oil and butter until soft and starting to colour. Add mushrooms and cook for a further 3 minutes. Add walnuts and cream and heat through. Season and mix with drained pasta.

Mushrooms and Almonds with Pasta
Serves 2

8 oz (200g) mushrooms, quartered
1 tablespoon (15ml) margarine
1 tablespoon (15ml) flour
5 fl oz (125ml) milk
pinch of mustard powder
black pepper
1 oz (25g) cheese, grated
6 oz (150g) pasta

Cook mushrooms in margarine for 5 minutes. Sprinkle in flour, and stir-fry for 1 minute. Slowly blend in milk. Cook until sauce thickens. Season with mustard powder and pepper and add cheese. Continue to cook until cheese melts. Meanwhile, cook pasta as directed on packet. When cooked, drain and mix with sauce.

Simple Spaghetti
Serves 2

> 8 oz (200g) spaghetti
> 1 clove garlic, crushed
> sprig rosemary, chopped
> 1 tablespoon (15ml) olive oil
> 14-oz (400-g) can chopped tomatoes
> knob of butter
> Parmesan, to serve

Cook spaghetti in boiling water. Meanwhile, gently cook garlic and rosemary in oil – do not brown. Add tomatoes and simmer until spaghetti is cooked. When spaghetti is ready, drain, add butter and then add sauce. Serve with Parmesan cheese.

Pasta with Sun-dried Tomatoes
Serves 2

> 8 oz (200g) pasta
> 4 sun-dried tomatoes in oil, drained and chopped
> 2 oz (50g) pitted black olives, chopped
> 2 tablespoons (30ml) olive oil

Cook pasta as directed on packet. When cooked and drained, mix in other ingredients and serve immediately.

Courgettes and Mushrooms with Pasta
Serves 2

    6 oz (150g) pasta spirals
    1 teaspoon (5ml) garlic purée
    4 oz (100g) courgettes, sliced
    4 oz (100g) mushrooms, sliced
    2 tablespoons (30ml) oil
    5 fl oz (125ml) stock
    1 tablespoon (15ml) pesto
    2 tablespoons (30ml) tomato purée
    2 tablespoons (30ml) Parmesan cheese

Cook pasta as directed on packet. Whilst cooking, fry garlic, courgettes and mushrooms in oil. Add rest of ingredients, except cheese, and bring to the boil. Cover and simmer gently for 5 minutes. Serve mixed into cooked, drained pasta and sprinkled with Parmesan. This is good with a watercress salad and garlic bread.

Pasta with Broccoli
Serves 2

    4 oz (100g) pasta
    1 onion, chopped
    1 clove garlic, crushed
    1 tablespoon (15ml) olive oil
    knob of butter
    6 oz (150g) broccoli, diced
    sprinkling of oregano
    black pepper

Cook pasta as directed on packet. Meanwhile, gently cook onion and garlic in oil until soft. Add butter and broccoli and continue to cook gently until pasta is ready. Add oregano and black pepper. Drain pasta and mix with this sauce.

Pasta Provençale
Serves 4

1 small aubergine, diced
1 red pepper, diced
1 green pepper, diced
2 cloves garlic, crushed
4 tablespoons (60ml) olive oil
14-oz (400-g) can or jar passata
1 tablespoon (15ml) tomato purée
sprinkling of basil
sprinkling of oregano
glass of red wine
1 lb (400g) spaghetti
2 oz (50g) pitted black olives, halved
Parmesan, to serve

Gently fry the aubergine, peppers and garlic in the oil until soft. Add passata and purée, herbs and red wine. Simmer for 30 minutes. When almost ready, cook spaghetti. When spaghetti is done, drain and serve with sauce and olives mixed on top. Sprinkle with Parmesan before serving.

Pasta Arrabbiata
Serves 2

6 oz (150g) spaghetti
1 red pepper, finely chopped
1 clove garlic, crushed
1 teaspoon (5ml) 'lazy' chilli
3 tablespoons (45ml) olive oil
7-oz (200-g) can chopped tomatoes
sprinkling of parsley, chopped

Cook spaghetti in boiling water. Meanwhile, cook pepper, garlic and chilli in oil until soft. Add tomatoes and parsley and simmer until spaghetti is cooked. Drain spaghetti and mix with sauce.

Pasta Alfredo
Serves 2

> 6 oz (150g) pasta
> 2 oz (50g) butter
> 5 fl oz (125ml) double cream
> 6 tablespoons (90ml) Parmesan cheese
> salt and pepper
> Parmesan, to serve

Cook pasta as directed on packet. Melt butter and add the rest of the ingredients, except for the final sprinkling of Parmesan. When pasta is cooked, drain and mix with sauce. Serve with more Parmesan.

Pasta Formaggio
Serves 2

> 1 oz (25g) butter
> 5 fl oz (125ml) single cream
> 2 oz (50g) Emmental cheese, grated
> 2 oz (50g) Gruyère cheese, grated
> 2 oz (50g) Mozzarella cheese, grated
> 2 tablespoons (30ml) Parmesan cheese
> 6 oz (150g) pasta quills (penne)

Melt butter. Add cream and cheeses and let these melt until you have a smooth sauce. Meanwhile, cook pasta as directed on packet. When cooked, drain and mix with sauce.

Lemony Beans with Pasta
Serves 2

1 onion, finely chopped
1 clove garlic, crushed
1 tablespoon (15ml) oil
grated rind of 1 lemon
2 teaspoons (10ml) lemon juice
1 teaspoon (5ml) sugar
5 fl oz (125ml) double cream
16-oz (400-g) can cannellini beans
4 oz (100g) pasta
sprinkling of parsley, chopped

Gently fry onion and garlic in oil. Add lemon rind and juice, sugar and cream, stirring whilst cooking. Add beans and heat through. Meanwhile, cook pasta as directed on packet. When cooked, drain and mix with bean sauce and parsley.

Mushroom Stroganoff
Serves 2

1 onion, finely chopped
1 green pepper, diced
1 clove garlic, crushed
1 tablespoon (15ml) oil
8 oz (200g) browncap mushrooms, quartered
knob of butter
1 tablespoon (15ml) plain flour
1 teaspoon (5ml) soy sauce
1 teaspoon (5ml) mushroom ketchup
2 tablespoons (30ml) dry white wine or sherry
4 tablespoons (60ml) sour cream
4 oz (100g) tagliatelle

Fry the onion, pepper and garlic in oil until soft. Add mushrooms and butter and cook for a further 5 minutes. Add rest of ingredients. Cook tagliatelle in boiling water. When pasta is cooked, drain and serve with sauce on top.

Cheesy Pasta
Serves 2

4 oz (100g) pasta
knob of butter
few spring onions, chopped
6 oz (150g) Ricotta cheese
black pepper
sprinkling of parsley, chopped
sprinkling of basil

Cook pasta as directed on packet. When cooked, drain, and on a gentle heat, add the other ingredients, mix and heat through. Serve immediately.

Pasta Neapolitan
Serves 2

6 oz (150g) pasta
2 cloves garlic, crushed
2 oz (50g) sun-dried tomatoes, chopped
1 tablespoon (15ml) olive oil
7-oz (200-g) can or jar passata
sprinkling of oregano
chopped olives (optional)
Parmesan cheese, to serve

Cook pasta as directed on packet. Meanwhile, cook garlic and sun-dried tomatoes in oil – do not brown. Add passata and oregano and simmer until pasta is ready. Drain pasta and mix with sauce and olives, if using. Serve with Parmesan cheese.

Pasta with Chilli Cheese Sauce
Serves 2

8 oz (200g) pasta
2 oz (50g) butter
8 oz (200g) Ricotta cheese
1 teaspoon (5ml) hot chilli sauce

Cook pasta as directed on packet. When cooked, drain and on a gentle heat mix with other ingredients and heat through. Serve immediately.

Pasta with Nutty Cauliflower Sauce
Serves 2

> 6 oz (150g) pasta
> 6 oz (150g) cauliflower, diced
> 2 tablespoons (30ml) olive oil
> 2 tablespoons (30ml) pine nuts
> 5 fl oz (125ml) double cream
> 2 tablespoons (30ml) Ricotta cheese
> sprinkling of basil
> Parmesan, to serve

Cook pasta as directed on packet. Fry cauliflower gently in oil until soft. Add nuts, cream, cheese and basil. Continue to cook gently until you have a thick sauce. Drain pasta and mix with sauce. Serve with Parmesan cheese.

Pasta with Mushrooms and Peas
Serves 2

> 6 oz (150g) pasta
> 8 oz (200g) browncap mushrooms, sliced
> 2 oz (50g) butter
> 1 teaspoon (5ml) mushroom ketchup
> 4 oz (100g) frozen peas
> dash of Tabasco sauce
> Parmesan cheese, to serve

Cook pasta as directed on packet. Whilst cooking, fry mushrooms gently in butter for 5 minutes. Add rest of ingredients, except for Parmesan, and stir-fry until pasta is cooked. Drain pasta and mix with vegetables. Serve with Parmesan cheese.

Potato Gnocchi with Tomato Sauce
Serves 4

  1 lb (400g) potatoes, cooked and mashed
  8 oz (200g) plain flour
  1 oz (25g) soft margarine or butter
  salt and pepper
  10 fl oz (250ml) tomato sauce (see p. 139)
  2 teaspoons (10ml) pesto
  Parmesan, to serve

Mix the potato, flour, and soft margarine or butter together and season well with the salt and pepper. Knead on a floured surface until dough feels elastic. Pull little even-sized pieces of dough off and shape into little rolls, flatten and then twist one end towards you. Cook in boiling, salted water for 8-10 minutes (try one to see if it is cooked). Heat the tomato sauce and add pesto. Serve gnocchi with tomato sauce poured over and Parmesan cheese sprinkled on top. Good with garlic bread.

Aubergine and Lentil Sauce for pasta
Serves 4

  1 onion, chopped
  1 teaspoon (5ml) garlic purée
  1 red pepper, chopped
  1 green pepper, chopped
  4 tablespoons (60ml) olive oil
  1 aubergine, diced
  8 oz (200g) red lentils
  10 fl oz (250ml) vegetable stock
  14-oz (400-g) can chopped tomatoes
  2 tablespoons (30ml) tomato purée
  1 tablespoon (15ml) pesto

Fry the onion, garlic and peppers in 2 tablespoons (30ml) of the oil. Add remaining oil and aubergine. Cook for 4 minutes. Add rest of ingredients, bring to the boil and then simmer gently for 20 minutes. Serve with spaghetti or jacket potatoes and salad.

Avocado and Banana with Pasta
Serves 2

> 6 oz (150g) pasta
> 2 small or 1 large ripe avocado
> 2 small or 1 large ripe banana
> 2 tablespoons (30ml) soft margarine
> 2 tablespoons (30ml) smooth peanut butter
> black pepper

Cook pasta in boiling water as directed on packet. While cooking pasta, peel, stone and chop avocado. Peel and chop banana. Beat together the margarine and peanut butter. When pasta is cooked, drain and add all other ingredients, seasoning with black pepper and mixing carefully. Put back on the heat briefly, to heat ingredients through. Serve immediately.

PIZZA

Pizza Dough

    4 oz (100g) strong white bread flour
    4 oz (100g) strong brown bread flour
    1 teaspoon (5ml) salt
    1 teaspoon (5ml) sugar
    1 teaspoon (5ml) easy blend yeast
    1 teaspoon (5ml) olive oil
    5 fl oz (125ml) hand-hot water

Mix all ingredients together, then knead for 5 minutes. Leave the dough to rise in a covered bowl for 45 minutes. Before using, knead once more until smooth.

Tomato Sauce
Makes 10 fl oz (250ml)

    1 garlic clove, chopped or crushed
    oil for frying
    14-oz (400-g) can chopped tomatoes
    1 tablespoon (15ml) tomato purée
    sprinkling of basil

Fry the garlic gently in the oil (if you can afford it, olive oil is the preferred oil for this dish). Now, add the rest of the ingredients and simmer very gently until the sauce is of the consistency that you want.

Pan Pizza
Serves 2

When you are in a hurry, this is the perfect quick pizza.

    6 oz (150g) self-raising flour
    1 teaspoon (5ml) salt
    4 teaspoons (20ml) oil
    oil for frying
    4 tablespoons (60ml) tomato purée
    1 tablespoon (15ml) pesto
    sprinkling of Parmesan

Mix flour, salt and oil together. Add enough water to make a soft dough – approximately 6 tablespoons (90ml). Knead and press out to fit a frying pan. Fry for 4 minutes over a medium heat, then turn and cook other side. Spread with tomato purée and pesto. Sprinkle with Parmesan. Grill for a few minutes under a hot grill.

Tomato and Pine Nut Pizza
Serves 2

    1 recipe pizza dough (see p. 139)
    10 fl oz (250ml) tomato sauce (see p. 139)
    4 oz (100g) sun-dried tomatoes in oil, chopped
    1 tablespoon (15ml) pine nuts
    sprinkling of basil
    1 oz (25g) Mozzarella cheese, grated
    black pepper

Pre-heat oven to 200°C/400°F/Gas 6. Roll out pizza dough to form base and prick all over with a fork. Spread with tomato sauce and then arrange tomatoes and pine nuts on top. Add basil – fresh herbs are best if you have them, otherwise use freeze-dried. Sprinkle with cheese and season with pepper. Bake on a pizza dish or baking tray in pre-heated oven for 25-30 minutes.

TOMATO AND OLIVE PIZZA
Follow recipe above, but substitute a handful of pitted olives, chopped, for the pine nuts.

Pizza with Peppers and Olives
Serves 2

    1 recipe pizza dough (see p. 139)
    10 fl oz (250ml) tomato sauce (see p. 139)
    1 red pepper, sliced
    1 clove garlic, crushed
    1 tablespoon (15ml) oil
    2 oz (50g) pitted black olives, halved
    sprinkling of oregano
    1 oz (25g) Mozzarella cheese, grated
    black pepper

Pre-heat oven to 200°C/400°F/Gas 6. Roll out pizza dough to form base and prick all over with fork. Spread with tomato sauce. Stir-fry pepper and garlic in oil for 2 minutes and then spoon onto pizza. Add olives and oregano and sprinkle with cheese. Season with black pepper and bake on a pizza dish or baking tray in pre-heated oven for 25-30 minutes.

Cheesy Pizza
Serves 2

    1 recipe pizza dough (see p. 139)
    10 fl oz (250ml) tomato sauce (see p. 139)
    4 oz (100g) Mozzarella cheese, sliced
    4 oz (100g) blue cheese, crumbled
    2 tablespoons (30ml) grated Parmesan cheese
    black pepper

Pre-heat oven to 200°C/400°F/Gas 6. Roll out pizza dough to form base and prick all over with a fork. Spread with tomato sauce. Arrange Mozzarella and blue cheese on pizza and sprinkle with Parmesan cheese. Season with pepper. Bake on a pizza dish or baking tray in pre-heated oven for 25-30 minutes.

Pizza with Four Cheeses
Serves 2

>1 recipe pizza dough (see p. 139)
>10 fl oz (250ml) tomato sauce (see p. 139)
>2 oz (50g) Mozzarella cheese, sliced
>2 oz (50g) Gruyère cheese, sliced
>2 oz (50g) Dolcelatte cheese, crumbled
>2 oz (50g) Austrian smoked cheese, sliced
>sprinkling of basil
>black pepper

Pre-heat oven to 200°C/400°F/Gas 6. Roll out pizza dough to form base and prick all over with a fork. Spread with tomato sauce and arrange a different cheese on each quarter of the pizza. Sprinkle with basil and season with pepper. Bake on a pizza dish or baking tray in pre-heated oven for 25-30 minutes.

Pizza Margherita
Serves 2

Although this classic pizza is extremely simple, it is also exceedingly delicious.

>1 recipe pizza dough (see p. 139)
>10 fl oz (250ml) tomato sauce (see p. 139)
>6 oz (150g) Mozzarella cheese, grated
>2 tablespoons (30ml) grated Parmesan cheese
>sprinkling of basil
>1 tablespoon (15ml) olive oil

Pre-heat oven to 200°C/400°F/Gas 6. Roll out pizza dough to form base and prick all over with a fork. Spread with tomato sauce. Sprinkle with cheeses and basil, and then drizzle oil over the top of the pizza. Bake on a pizza dish or baking tray in pre-heated oven for 25-30 minutes.

Deep Pan Pizza
Serves 2

Forget the takeaway – make your own version of deep pan pizza!

    1 recipe pizza dough (see p. 139)
    10 fl oz (250ml) tomato sauce (see p. 139)
    sprinkling of pitted black olives, sliced
    sprinkling of basil
    sprinkling of oregano
    sprinkling of rosemary
    4 oz (100g) Mozzarella cheese, sliced
    black pepper

Pre-heat oven to 200°C/400°F/Gas 6. Roll out pizza dough to fit an 8 in (20cm) flan tin or deep pie dish. Spread with the tomato sauce and sprinkle with olives and herbs. Arrange slices of cheese on top and season with pepper. Cook in pre-heated oven for 25-30 minutes.

Mushroom Pizza
Serves 2

> 1 recipe pizza dough (see p. 139)
> 10 fl oz (250ml) tomato sauce (see p. 139)
> 4 oz (100g) browncap mushrooms, sliced
> 1 clove garlic, crushed
> 1 tablespoon (15ml) olive oil
> 2 oz (50g) Mozzarella cheese, grated
> sprinkling of oregano
> black pepper

Pre-heat oven to 200°C/400°F/Gas 6. Roll out pizza dough to form base and prick all over with a fork. Spread with tomato sauce. Stir-fry mushrooms and garlic in oil for 2 minutes, and then spoon over pizza base. Sprinkle with cheese and oregano and season with pepper. Bake on a pizza dish or baking tray in pre-heated oven for 25-30 minutes.

Pizza Mexicana
Serves 2

> 1 recipe pizza dough (see p. 139)
> 10 fl oz (250ml) tomato sauce (see p. 139)
> 2 tablespoons (30ml) canned red kidney beans, drained
> half an avocado, cubed
> sprinkling of oregano
> good dash of Tabasco sauce
> 3 oz (75g) Mozzarella cheese, grated

Pre-heat oven to 200°C/400°F/Gas 6. Roll out pizza dough to form base and prick all over with fork. Spread with tomato sauce and top with beans and avocado. Sprinkle with oregano, Tabasco sauce and cheese. Bake on a pizza dish or baking tray in pre-heated oven for 25-30 minutes.

Pizza Genoese
Serves 2

> 1 recipe pizza dough (see p. 139)
> 10 fl oz (250ml) tomato sauce (see p. 139)
> 2 tablespoons (30ml) pesto
> sprinkling of basil
> 1 tablespoon (15ml) pine nuts
> 2 canned artichoke hearts, sliced
> 2 tablespoons (30ml) grated Parmesan cheese
> black pepper

Pre-heat oven to 200°C/400°F/Gas 6. Roll out pizza dough to form base and prick all over with a fork. Mix the tomato sauce and pesto together and spread over pizza base. Sprinkle with basil and pine nuts and arrange slices of artichoke hearts on pizza. Sprinkle with Parmesan and season with pepper. Bake on a pizza dish or baking tray in pre-heated oven for 25-30 minutes.

Calzoni
Serves 2

> 1 recipe pizza dough (see p. 139)
> 1 tablespoon (15ml) pesto
> 4 oz (100g) Ricotta cheese
> 2 oz (50g) Mozzarella cheese, grated
> 1 egg, beaten
> black pepper

Pre-heat oven to 200°C/400°F/Gas 6. Divide pizza dough into two. Roll each out into a circle. Mix together the other ingredients and divide between the two circles. Fold each circle into half, enclosing the mixture, and seal edges. Bake on a baking tray in pre-heated oven for 25-30 minutes.

Pizza Lucia
Serves 2

Those of you who have read (and used) *Grub on a Grant*
may remember my friend Lucy, with whom I shared a flat
and many milk bottles (but that's another story!). This is a
recipe passed to me from her – thus the name.

> 1 recipe pizza dough (see p. 139)
> 10 fl oz (250ml) tomato sauce (see p. 139)
> 1 tablespoon (15ml) red pesto
> 2 tablespoons (30ml) chopped pineapple
> 2 tablespoons (30ml) canned sweetcorn
> sprinkling of basil
> dash of Tabasco sauce
> 3 oz (75g) Austrian smoked cheese, sliced
> black pepper

Pre-heat oven to 200°C/400°F/Gas 6. Roll out pizza dough to
form base and prick all over with a fork. Spread with tomato
sauce. Mix pesto with pineapple and sweetcorn and spoon
over pizza. Sprinkle with basil and Tabasco, then arrange
cheese on top. Season with pepper and bake on a pizza dish
or baking tray in pre-heated oven for 25-30 minutes.

8 Curries

Of course, there is really no such dish as a curry – not in India, anyway! However, it has become the term for many spiced dishes, and although curries can differ enormously, people always know what you mean if you talk of 'having a curry'. There have been many cookery books written about vegetarian curries, so I have only given a few recipes here – enough just to tempt the palate. Many people who are unaware of what Indian cuisine is all about believe that curries have to be 'hot'. This is certainly not so. It is the flavouring that is important, not the heat. It is this flavouring that produces the many different types of curries, each using different spices and herbs. However, if you only want to try these dishes out from time to time, you will not want to collect a whole cupboard of different flavourings – especially as they are likely to go past their best before you get round to using them up.

Therefore, I suggest that you only keep coriander and cumin in your cupboard, and buy a couple of universal flavourings that you can use to base your curries on. Garam masala is very useful, as is, depending on your own preference, a 'korma' or 'madras' curry powder.

You will find that there are many different types on offer, available either as powders or pastes. If you buy a powder, you often need to make it into a paste to use it. To do this just mix it with a teaspoon of groundnut oil and a little water. This is then added to the fried onions that all curries are based on, and fried for a few minutes. This procedure ensures that the spices are cooked, and so will give your curry its lovely taste at the end of its cooking time.

Curries should be served with basmati rice or Indian breads. I also like to serve raita and Indian chutneys, and sometimes onion bhajees or samosas.

Spinach and Lentil Curry
Serves 2

1 onion, chopped
1 clove garlic, crushed
1 tablespoon (15ml) oil
1 tablespoon (15ml) curry paste
1 teaspoon (5ml) 'lazy' chilli
4 oz (100g) lentils
15 fl oz (375ml) water
8 oz (200g) spinach, chopped
7-oz (200-g) can chopped tomatoes
5 fl oz (125ml) Greek yoghurt
sprinkling of coriander

Fry onion and garlic in oil until soft. Add curry paste and chilli and cook for 1 minute. Add lentils and water. Cook for 10 minutes. Add spinach and cover and cook for 5 minutes. When water has been absorbed, mix in tomatoes and yoghurt and heat through. Serve with a sprinkling of coriander and rice.

Chickpea and Mushroom Curry
Serves 2

This is a really nice curry. I have found that the addition of creamed coconut gives curries a rich, creamy consistency.

1 onion, chopped
1 clove garlic, crushed
1 tablespoon (15ml) oil
4 oz (100g) mushrooms, quartered
1 oz (25g) creamed coconut
1 tablespoon (15ml) curry paste
1 tablespoon (15ml) tomato purée
16-oz (400g) can chickpeas, drained
10 fl oz (250ml) Greek yoghurt

Fry onion and garlic in oil until soft. Add mushrooms and cook for a further 5 minutes. Mix coconut to a paste with some boiling water, and add curry paste and tomato purée. Add to vegetables and cook for 1 minute. Add chickpeas and yoghurt and heat through. Serve with rice.

Bean Dopiaza
Serves 2

> 2 onions
> 2 tablespoons (30ml) oil
> 2 teaspoons (10ml) garlic purée
> 2 teaspoons (10ml) ginger purée
> 16-oz (400-g) can black-eyed beans, drained
> 1 tablespoon (15ml) curry paste
> 1 tablespoon (15ml) soft margarine or butter
> 5 fl oz (125ml) Greek yoghurt
> lemon juice

Cut 1 onion in half lengthways and then cut each half into quarters. Fry onion in 1 tablespoon (15ml) oil with half of garlic and ginger purées until soft. Add beans. Finely chop other onion. In another pan, heat rest of oil and add the remaining onion, the rest of the garlic and ginger purées, the curry paste, and the margarine or butter. Add yoghurt and lemon juice to taste, ensuring that this mixture does not boil. Mix all ingredients together. Serve with rice and poppadoms.

Mushroom Korma
Serves 2

> 1 onion, chopped
> 1 teaspoon (15ml) garlic purée
> 1 teaspoon (15ml) ginger purée
> 1 tablespoon (15ml) mild curry paste
> 1 tablespoon (15ml) oil
> 8 oz (200g) browncap mushrooms, left whole
> 1 tablespoon (15ml) soft margarine or butter
> 8 fl oz (200ml) Greek yoghurt
> 1 tablespoon (15ml) ground almonds
> 1 tablespoon (15ml) lemon juice

Fry the onion, garlic and ginger purées, and curry paste in oil until soft. Add mushrooms to pan with margarine or butter and continue to cook for 5 minutes. Add other ingredients and stir well. Cover tightly and simmer very gently for 5 minutes. Serve with shelled pistachio nuts, chopped finely, and rice and poppadoms.

Circassia Beans
Serves 2

> 4 oz (100g) ground walnuts
> 3 oz (75g) white breadcrumbs
> 1 tablespoon (15ml) curry paste
> sprinkling of cayenne pepper
> boiling vegetable stock
> 2 oz (50g) butter, melted
> 16-oz (400-g) can cannellini beans, drained

Mix the nuts, breadcrumbs, curry paste and cayenne pepper together in a saucepan. Mix in enough vegetable stock to make a walnut sauce. Mix the butter and beans together and add to the sauce. Warm through and serve with rice.

Vegetable and Lentil Curry
Serves 2

> 1 onion, chopped
> 1 carrot, diced
> 1 clove garlic, crushed
> 1 tablespoon (15ml) oil
> 1 teaspoon (5ml) ginger purée
> 1 tablespoon (15ml) curry paste
> 7-oz (200-g) can chopped tomatoes
> 1 tablespoon (15ml) tomato purée
> 4 oz (100g) red split lentils
> 4 oz (100g) cauliflower, diced
> 15 fl oz (375ml) vegetable stock

Fry the onion, carrot and garlic in oil until soft. Add ginger and curry paste and fry for 1 minute. Add rest of ingredients and bring to the boil. Cover and simmer for 15-20 minutes until you have a thick curry.

Vegetable Biryani
Serves 2

> 2 tablespoons (30ml) curry paste
> 2 teaspoons (10ml) garlic purée
> 2 teaspoons (10ml) ginger purée
> 8 oz (200g) basmati rice
> 3 tablespoons (45ml) oil
> pinch of cumin seeds
> sprinkling of sultanas
> 15 fl oz (375ml) boiling vegetable stock
> 1 onion, chopped
> 1 tablespoon (15ml) soft margarine or butter
> mixture of vegetables, e.g. cauliflower florets, courgette
>   chunks, carrot sticks, peas
> 14-oz (400-g) can chopped tomatoes
> sprinkling of pistachio nuts or almonds

Gently fry half each of the curry paste, garlic and ginger with all of the rice in 1 tablespoon (15ml) of oil. Add the cumin seeds, sultanas and stock. Stir, then cover and leave to simmer gently for 20 minutes. Meanwhile, in another pan gently fry the remaining curry paste, garlic and ginger and the onion in another tablespoon (15ml) oil and soft margarine or butter. Add your vegetables and quickly stir-fry them. Add the tomatoes and simmer gently until rice is ready. Stir the remaining oil and the nuts into the rice, then serve with vegetable curry. Good with poppadoms and lime chutney.

Kitcheree
Serves 2

    1 onion, chopped
    2 tablespoons (30ml) groundnut oil
    sprinkling of curry powder
    4 oz (100g) long grain rice
    4 oz (100g) split red lentils
    boiling water

Fry onion in oil until soft. Add curry powder and stir-fry for 1 minute. Add the rice and lentils and stir-fry for another minute. Cover with boiling water. Cover and simmer for 20 minutes or until the water is absorbed.

Mixed Vegetable Curry
Serves 2

    12 oz (300g) potatoes, cubed
    4 oz (100g) carrots, diced
    6 oz (150g) cauliflower, chopped
    3 tablespoons (45ml) groundnut oil
    1 tablespoons (15ml) curry paste
    4 oz (100g) peas
    7-oz (200-g) can chopped tomatoes
    5 fl oz (125ml) water
    2 tablespoons (30ml) Greek yoghurt

Cook the potatoes and carrots in boiling water for 5 minutes and then drain. Fry with the cauliflower in oil for 5 minutes. Add the curry paste and stir-fry for 2 minutes. Add peas, tomatoes and water. Bring to the boil, cover and simmer gently for 5 minutes. Just before serving stir in yoghurt and gently heat through.

Lentil Dhal
Serves 2

1 onion, chopped
2 tablespoons (30ml) groundnut oil
6 oz (150g) red split lentils
1 teaspoons (5ml) curry paste
1 teaspoon (5ml) cumin
1 pint (500ml) boiling water
1 tablespoon (15ml) butter
sprinkling of coriander

Fry the onion in oil until soft. Add the lentils, curry paste and cumin and stir-fry for 2 minutes. Add the water, and simmer until it is absorbed. Before serving stir in butter and sprinkle with coriander.

Bombay Vegetables
Serves 2

1 onion, chopped
1 clove garlic, crushed
4 tablespoons (60ml) oil
1 teaspoon (5ml) black mustard seeds
2 tablespoons (30ml) curry paste
2 carrots, grated
8 oz (200g) potatoes, cooked and drained
4 oz (100g) cauliflower, diced
10 fl oz (250ml) Greek yoghurt

Fry onion and garlic in oil until soft. Add mustard seeds and fry until they 'pop'. Add curry paste and cook for 1 minute. Add rest of ingredients and heat through.

Nutty Cauliflower Curry
Serves 2

> 1 onion, chopped
> 1 tablespoon (15ml) 'lazy' garlic
> 1 tablespoon (15ml) 'lazy' ginger
> 2 tablespoons (30ml) oil
> 1 teaspoon (5ml) curry paste
> 8 oz (200g) cauliflower florets
> 10 fl oz (250ml) boiling water
> 1 tablespoon (15ml) ground almonds
> 2 oz (50g) cashew nuts
> 4 tablespoons (100ml) Greek yoghurt
> sprinkling of coriander

Cook onion, garlic and ginger in oil until soft. Add curry paste and cauliflower and stir-fry for 2 minutes. Add boiling water, cover and cook for 8 minutes. Stir in other ingredients and heat through.

Simple Vegetable Bhajee
Serves 2

> 12 oz (300g) new potatoes, quartered
> 1 onion, chopped
> 1 teaspoon (5ml) 'lazy' garlic
> 1 teaspoon (5ml) 'lazy' ginger
> 2 tablespoons (30ml) oil
> 1 tablespoon (15ml) coriander
> 1 tablespoon (15ml) cumin
> dash of chilli sauce
> 6 oz (150g) cauliflower florets
> 4 oz (100g) peas
> 7-oz (200-g) can chopped tomatoes
> 10 fl oz (250ml) boiling water

Boil the potatoes for 10 minutes and then drain. Fry onion, garlic and ginger in oil until soft. Add coriander, cumin and chilli sauce and stir-fry for 1 minute. Add cauliflower and peas and stir-fry for a further minute. Add tomatoes and water, cover and cook for 10 minutes.

Indian Vegetables
Serves 2

> 1 onion, chopped
> 4 oz (100g) potatoes, cooked
> 4 oz (100g) cauliflower, diced
> 1 carrot, diced
> 4 tablespoons (60ml) oil
> 1 oz (25g) creamed coconut
> 1 teaspoon (5ml) chilli powder
> sprinkling of cumin
> sprinkling of coriander
> 5 fl oz (125ml) Greek yoghurt

Fry vegetables in oil until starting to brown. Mix coconut to a paste with some boiling water. Mix in spices. Add to vegetables and stir-fry for 2 minutes. Add yoghurt and heat through.

Hot and Sour Curry
Serves 2

1 onion, sliced
4 tablespoons (60ml) groundnut oil
1 aubergine, diced
1 teaspoon (5ml) 'lazy' ginger
1 teaspoon (5ml) 'lazy' chilli
1 teaspoon (5ml) coriander
1 teaspoon (5ml) cumin
1 teaspoon (5ml) cinnamon
2 tablespoons (30ml) vinegar
1 tablespoon (15ml) muscovado sugar
10 fl oz (250ml) boiling water

Fry the onion in oil until brown. Add aubergine and stir-fry for 2-3 minutes. Add spices and continue frying for 1 minute. Add the vinegar and sugar and stir until sugar melts. Add water, cover and cook for 20 minutes or until aubergine is cooked.

Okra and Peanut Curry
Serves 2

1 onion, chopped
1 clove garlic, chopped or crushed
1 tablespoon (15ml) oil
2 oz (50g) creamed coconut
1 tablespoon (15ml) Thai 7-spice seasoning
2 oz (50g) peanuts
8 oz (200g) okra, chopped
10 fl oz (250ml) orange juice

Fry onion and garlic in oil until browning. Make up the creamed coconut to a thick paste with hot water. Blend or purée the coconut, Thai seasoning and peanuts. Add with other ingredients to the pan and cook over a gentle heat until the okra is cooked through (about 20 minutes). Serve with rice or naan bread.

9 On the Side

There are many dishes that do not seem complete unless they are served with accompaniments. For me, these include raita and chutneys with curries, gravy or sauces with roasts, croûtons with soups, and, with many different dishes – garlic bread.

Side dishes or accompaniments are also very useful when making light lunches or for serving as a first course when entertaining. I am sure that you will find some of your favourites that you have enjoyed when eating at restaurants here. Why not have a go at making them yourself – a much cheaper option than buying supermarket versions.

White Sauce
Makes 10 fl oz (250ml)

> 1 oz (25g) butter or margarine
> 1 oz (25g) flour, sifted
> 10 fl oz (250ml) milk

Melt the butter or margarine in a small saucepan and then take the pan away from the heat. Add the flour, stir well and return to a gentle heat, stirring continuously. Add a little of the milk, and keep stirring to ensure lumps do not appear. The mixture will be very thick – keep thinning it gradually with the milk. When all of the milk has been incorporated, keep stirring and continue cooking for a minute or two to ensure that the flour is cooked through.

This sauce can be used in a number of ways, e.g.

CHEESE
Add 2 oz (50g) grated cheese to the sauce and a touch of mustard.

PARSLEY
Add 2 tablespoons (30ml) chopped fresh parsley, with salt and pepper to taste.

MUSHROOM
Add 4 oz (100g) sliced mushrooms and 1 tablespoon (15ml) double cream.

Add the various extra ingredients when all the milk has been incorporated.

Onion Gravy
Serves 2

1 onion, chopped
1 tablespoon (15ml) oil
1 tablespoon (15ml) butter
1 tablespoon (15ml) plain flour
1 teaspoon (5ml) mushroom ketchup
few drops of gravy browning
10 fl oz (250ml) boiling vegetable stock

Fry the onion in the oil and butter until browning. Stir in the flour and cook for 1 minute. Add the mushroom ketchup and the gravy browning. Gradually blend in the stock and let simmer for 5 minutes.

Marinated Mushrooms
Serves 2

3 tablespoons (45ml) olive oil
1 tablespoon (15ml) red wine vinegar
1 teaspoon (5ml) caster sugar
1 tablespoon (15ml) tomato purée
4 oz (100g) mushrooms, sliced

Blend together the oil, vinegar, sugar and tomato purée. Mix with the mushrooms and leave to stand for at least one hour before serving.

Spicy Sauté
Serves 2

1 onion, finely chopped
1 red pepper, diced
2 sticks celery, sliced
2 tablespoons (30ml) olive oil
1 tablespoon (15ml) tomato purée
2 teaspoons (10ml) brown sugar
1 tablespoon (15ml) red wine vinegar
dash of Tabasco sauce

Fry the onion, pepper and celery in the oil until soft. Add all other ingredients and cook for a few minutes. Leave to cool before serving.

Potato Pancakes
Serves 2

>8 oz (200g) potato, grated
>1 tablespoon (15ml) plain flour
>salt and pepper
>sprinkling of paprika
>1 egg, beaten
>oil for frying

Mix potato with flour, seasonings and egg. In a large frying pan, heat some oil. Drop tablespoons of the potato mixture into the hot oil, flattening it into a 'cake'. Fry for a few minutes and then turn so that it browns on both sides.

Red Pepper Butter
Serves 2

>1 red pepper, diced
>4 oz (100g) butter, softened
>1 tablespoon (15ml) tomato purée

Blend all ingredients. Form into a tube shape and wrap in greaseproof paper. Freeze until required. Cut into rounds to serve. I add this to stir-fries and soups to add pungency.

Red Pepper Sauce
Serves 2

>2 red peppers, diced
>1 onion, finely chopped
>1 clove garlic, crushed
>2 tablespoons (30ml) oil
>7-oz (200-g) can chopped tomatoes
>sprinkling of Tabasco sauce

Fry peppers, onion and garlic in oil until soft. Blend with tomatoes and return to heat. Add Tabasco and simmer for 10 minutes before serving. This is great for jazzing up roasts and pies.

Rouille

2 oz (50g) fresh breadcrumbs, soaked in water
1 clove garlic, crushed
½ teaspoon (2.5ml) 'lazy' chilli or chopped red chilli
1 tablespoon (15ml) tomato purée
2 tablespoons (30ml) olive oil

Squeeze out excess water from bread, then mash all ingredients together. This produces a lovely chilli sauce which you can add to soups to increase their ferocity!

Home-made Croûtons

These can be made in a number of ways, and can also be varied by using differently flavoured oils and herbs when making them.

In each instance you will need for each serving:

1 tablespoon (15ml) oil
1 oz (25g) stale bread, cubed
sprinkling of herbs

To fry croûtons, heat the oil and add small cubes of the bread. Flavour with herbs and stir-fry until bread is crisp and brown. Transfer to kitchen paper to absorb any excess oil.

To bake croûtons, pre-heat oven to 180°C/350°F/Gas 4. Place the oil, cubed bread, and herbs in a bowl and mix well. Leave bread to absorb oil. Then spread over a baking tray and cook in pre-heated oven for 5-10 minutes until brown and crispy.

To grill croûtons, prepare them as for baking but cook instead under a hot grill, stirring occasionally. They need careful watching when being done under the grill, as they burn easily.

Croûtons can be left for about 1 week in an air-tight container.

Garlic Bread

> 1 French baguette
> 4 oz (100g) softened butter
> 2 cloves garlic, crushed
> 1 tablespoon (15ml) fresh parsley, chopped

Pre-heat oven to 160°C/325°F/Gas 3. Cut the bread into thick slices without completely separating each slice. Cream the butter with the garlic and parsley, and spread on each sliced side. Wrap bread loosely in foil and bake in pre-heated oven for 15 minutes. Fold foil back from bread, raise oven temperature to 220°C/425°F/Gas 7, and cook for a further 10 minutes or until crisp.

Batter

> 4 oz (100g) flour
> pinch of salt
> 1 egg, beaten
> 10 fl oz (250ml) milk

Put the flour and salt into a bowl. Make a well in the middle and put eggs and a little milk in this. Gradually beat liquid into flour. Add the rest of the milk a little at a time until you have a smooth batter. (Alternatively, put everything into a blender and just whizz together.)

Vegetable Fritters
Serves 2

> 10 fl oz (250ml) batter (see p. 164)
> mixed fresh vegetables, e.g. cauliflower or broccoli
>   florets, aubergine slices, courgette sticks
> fat, for frying

Heat the oil until it reaches 190°C/375°F, then dip vegetables in batter and fry for a few minutes until brown and crisp. Serve with tomato sauce or mango chutney.

Cheese Croquettes
Serves 2

> 8 oz (200g) cooked rice
> 2 oz (50g) cheese, grated
> 2 oz (50g) chopped mixed nuts
> 1 teaspoon (5ml) tomato purée
> sprinkling of Tabasco sauce
> 1 egg, beaten
> dried breadcrumbs
> oil, for frying

Mix all ingredients except breadcrumbs and oil together. Shape into little rolls. Coat in breadcrumbs and fry in oil until golden brown. Serve with tomato ketchup or chutney and a salad.

Breaded Mushrooms
Serves 2

> 4 oz (100g) button mushrooms
> 1 egg white, lightly beaten
> dried breadcrumbs
> oil, for frying

Dip mushrooms into egg white and then into breadcrumbs. Heat the oil to 190°C/375°F. Cook coated mushrooms for a few minutes in hot oil, until crisp and golden. Drain on paper towels.

Onion Bhajees
Serves 2

3 oz (75g) plain flour
1 tablespoon (15ml) cornflour
1 teaspoon (5ml) coriander
1 teaspoon (5ml) cumin
pinch of chilli powder
5 fl oz (125ml) warm water
1 onion, finely chopped
oil, for frying

Mix together the flours, spices and onion. Add enough of the water to make a thick batter. Heat the oil to 190°C/375°F and drop small balls of batter into the hot oil. Cook for about 8 minutes, until crisp and golden. Drain on kitchen paper before serving.

Raita
Serves 2

5 fl oz (125ml) natural yoghurt
pinch of salt
2 in (5cm) cucumber, finely chopped
1 teaspoon (5ml) mint, chopped
pinch of coriander

Mix all ingredients together. Raita can be garnished with whole mint or coriander leaves. You can add crushed garlic or chopped spring onions for a stronger flavour.

Vegetable Samosas
Serves 2

These are incredibly easy to make – I know because even Andy can make them!

> 4 oz (100g) potatoes, cubed
> 4 oz (100g) peas
> 4 oz (100g) self-raising flour
> 2 oz (50g) soft margarine or butter
> sprinkling of curry powder
> salt and pepper
> fat, for frying

Boil potatoes and peas until cooked and soft. Mix the flour and margarine into a dough, using some cold water to bind together. Divide dough into four small balls. Roll out in circles and cut each circle in half. Mix curry powder and salt and pepper into potato and pea mixture and place some of mixture in middle of each semicircle. Wet one corner of dough with water and fold over to form a triangle shape, then fold over other side and press edges together to seal. Fry in hot fat for a few minutes to brown all sides. Serve with mango chutney and salad.

Banana Chutney
Serves 2

> 1 banana, finely diced
> 1 teaspoon (5ml) sherry vinegar
> pinch of sugar
> dash of Tabasco sauce

Mix all ingredients together well. Leave to stand for 30 minutes before serving.

Garlic Sauce
Serves 2

> 5 fl oz (125ml) Greek yoghurt
> 2 cloves garlic, crushed
> salt and pepper

Mix all ingredients together and leave to stand for 30 minutes before using.

Jacket Potatoes
Serves 2

> 2 x 8 oz (200g) potatoes

Pre-heat oven to 200°C/400°F/Gas 6. Do not peel potatoes. Ensure that they are clean and rub well with oil. Cook in pre-heated oven for 75 minutes.

Crispy Potato Skins
Serves 2

> 8 oz (200g) thickly peeled potato skins
> 1 tablespoon (15ml) groundnut oil
> 2 tablespoons (30ml) soy sauce
> 1 teaspoon (5ml) paprika
> dash of Tabasco sauce
> pinch of salt

Mix all ingredients together and leave for 30 minutes to blend flavours. Meanwhile, pre-heat oven to 220°C/425°F/Gas 7. Place marinated potato skins on a baking tray and cook in pre-heated oven for 15-20 minutes, until crisp.

Guacamole
Serves 2

    1 ripe avocado
    1 clove garlic, crushed
    2 oz (50g) onion or spring onion, chopped
    squeeze of lemon or lime juice
    dash of Tabasco or chilli sauce
    pinch of coriander
    some chopped tomato or red pepper (optional)

Remove the skin and stone from the avocado and mash well. Mix with the rest of ingredients and serve immediately. As well as accompanying Mexican dishes such as refried beans or chills, guacamole can also be used as a dip.

Refried Beans
Serves 2

    4 oz (100g) pinto beans
    1 onion, chopped
    1 clove garlic, crushed
    3 tablespoons (45ml) groundnut oil
    salt and pepper
    sprinkling of Tabasco sauce

Soak beans overnight. Cook in boiling water (do not add salt to the cooking water) for 10 minutes, then simmer for 50 minutes until beans are cooked. Drain and mash beans roughly. Fry the onion and garlic in the oil until browning. Add the beans and stir-fry for 2-3 minutes. Season to taste. Use to fill burritos or tacos.

Salsa Sauce
Serves 2

>1 onion, chopped
>1 clove garlic, crushed
>1 teaspoon (5ml) 'lazy' chilli
>4 tablespoons (60ml) groundnut oil
>14-oz (400-g) can chopped tomatoes
>2 tablespoons (30ml) tomato purée
>1 teaspoon (5ml) sugar
>2 teaspoons (10ml) red wine vinegar

Fry onion, garlic and chilli in oil until soft. Add all other ingredients and simmer for 10 minutes.

Aubergine Fritters
Serves 2

>4 oz (100g) plain flour
>pinch of salt
>2 tablespoons (30ml) oil
>4 fl oz (100ml) warm water
>1 egg white, beaten
>1 aubergine, sliced
>oil, for frying

Blend together the flour, salt and oil. Gradually stir in the warm water and then beat in the egg white. Dip aubergine slices in this batter and then drop into hot oil. Fry for a few minutes, until brown on both sides – don't overcrowd the pan. Drain on paper towels, and serve with a sauce.

Note
To ring the changes, you can also use this batter to make **Onion Rings**. Just use thickly sliced onion instead of the aubergine.

Fried Onions
Serves 2

> 1 large onion, sliced
> knob of butter
> 1 teaspoon (5ml) brown sugar
> 1 teaspoon (5ml) vinegar

Fry onion in the butter until starting to brown. Add sugar and vinegar and stir-fry until onion is almost black.

Chips
Serves 2

> 12 oz (300g) potatoes
> oil, for frying

Peel potatoes and cut into slices, then cut each slice into strips. Wash and then dry well. Pre-heat oil to 190°C/375°F. Cook potato chips for 8 minutes in pre-heated oil until golden brown. Drain on paper towels.

Hummus
Serves 2

Hummus is a very useful dish – you can add a little more yoghurt and serve it with pasta, or it makes a useful lunch or supper snack. It is also a popular dish to use as a starter for dinner parties – when I decorate it with a sprinkling of paprika and serve it with some parsley and a wedge of lemon to accompany the pitta bread or toast.

> 16-oz (400-g) can chickpeas, drained
> sprinkling of cumin powder
> 2 cloves garlic, crushed
> pinch of salt
> 1 tablespoon (15ml) oil
> juice of half a lemon
> 2 tablespoons (30ml) Greek yoghurt
> black pepper

Put all ingredients in a liquidiser or blender and whizz. Serve with toast or pitta bread.

10 Sweet Things

Although we are not great fans of desserts in our household, there are times when one does fancy something sweet. So I have included here some of the recipes for puddings, cakes and biscuits that we do make occasionally.

Most vegetarian cookery books seem to specify wholemeal flours for cakes and biscuits. However, I find that some recipes are much nicer when ordinary flours are used, and therefore you will find recipes here for both types of flour. The emphasis in most vegetarian books is on healthy baking, but again I have found that my friends, although enjoying such things as flapjacks or muesli bars, tend to prefer rather naughtier treats! Of course, when entertaining we do offer our guests a dessert (or two), so I have included two of my most popular dinner party desserts – banoffee pie and mud pie. Both are very, very rich but absolutely divine!

Rhubarb Charlotte

1 lb (400g) rhubarb, cleaned and cubed
3 oz (75g) unsalted butter
6 oz (150g) fresh wholemeal breadcrumbs
1 teaspoon (5ml) mixed spice
2 oz (50g) brown sugar
2 tablespoons (30ml) orange juice
2 tablespoons (30ml) runny honey

Pre-heat oven to 200°C/400°F/Gas 6. Fry the rhubarb gently in half of the butter until soft. Remove from the pan. Fry the breadcrumbs in remaining butter until butter is absorbed and breadcrumbs are brown. Layer the rhubarb and breadcrumbs into an ovenproof dish, finishing with a layer of breadcrumbs. Mix rest of ingredients together and spoon over breadcrumbs. Bake in pre-heated oven for 20 minutes or until top is brown.

Note
You can also make **Blackberry Charlotte** by replacing the rhubarb with 1 lb (400g) blackberries. As you do not need to fry the blackberries you will only need half the amount of butter.

Lemon Meringue Pie

    12 oz (300g) shortcrust pastry (see p. 66)
    3 tablespoons (45ml) cornflour
    5 fl oz (125ml) water
    grated rind and juice of 2 lemons
    7 oz (175g) caster sugar
    2 eggs, separated

Pre-heat oven to 220°C/425°C/Gas 7. Roll out pastry to fit an 8 in (20cm) pie dish. Place a sheet of greaseproof paper inside and some coins. Bake in pre-heated oven for 15 minutes. Remove paper and coins. Blend together the cornflour and water, put into a small pan with lemon rind and juice, and bring to boil, stirring. Reduce heat and add 4 oz (100g) sugar. When sugar has dissolved, remove from heat and cool slightly. Beat the egg yolks and add to lemon mixture. Spoon into pastry case. Beat egg whites with half of remaining sugar. When stiff, fold in rest of sugar and pile meringue onto lemon filling. Bake in the oven for 10-15 minutes until meringue is crisp and lightly browned.

Note
To make **Key Lime Pie** replace the pastry base with a base made with 3 oz (75g) melted butter and 6 oz (150g) digestive or ginger snap biscuit crumbs mixed together and chilled instead of cooked. Replace the 2 lemons with 2 limes.

Syrup and Stem Ginger Cake

1 teaspoon (5ml) bicarbonate of soda
5 fl oz (125ml) milk
4 oz (100g) soft margarine
6 tablespoons (90ml) golden syrup
8 oz (200g) plain flour
1 teaspoon (5ml) mixed spice
2 eggs, beaten
2 tablespoons (30ml) soft brown sugar
8 pieces stem ginger, chopped
1 tablespoon (15ml) preserving sugar

Pre-heat oven to 160°C/325°F/Gas 3. Dissolve bicarbonate of soda in milk. Beat together all ingredients except preserving sugar and spoon into a greased, lined 2 lb (800g) loaf tin. Sprinkle with preserving sugar. Bake in pre-heated oven for 1 hour.

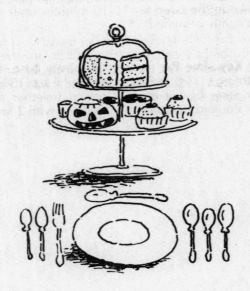

Orange Syrup Cake

8 oz (200g) soft margarine
8 oz (200g) caster sugar
4 eggs, beaten
2 tablespoons (30ml) ground rice
8 oz (200g) plain flour
2 tablespoons (30ml) baking powder
grated rind of 2 oranges
5 fl oz (125ml) fresh orange juice
3 oz (75g) icing sugar

Pre-heat oven to 180°C/350°F/Gas 4. Beat together all ingredients except orange juice and icing sugar. Spoon the mixture into a greased, lined 2 lb (800g) loaf tin. Bake in pre-heated oven for 75 minutes. Heat the orange juice with the icing sugar in a small pan. Pierce the cake in several places with a sharp skewer, and slowly pour the syrup over the cake until it is absorbed. Leave the cake in the tin overnight, before removing and serving.

I first had this cake when visiting our friend Mandy. Of course, time being of the essence, she was still baking the cake when I arrived. However, we proved that it could be eaten warm with the syrup poured over it. In fact, it was so good that we ate half of it before I left!

Marmalade Cake

    8 oz (200g) self-raising flour
    4 oz (100g) caster sugar
    4 oz (100g) soft margarine or butter
    4 oz (100g) marmalade
    2 eggs, beaten
    4 tablespoons (60ml) milk

Pre-heat oven to 180°C/350°F/Gas 4. Beat all ingredients together and spoon into a lined 1 lb (400g) loaf tin. Cook in pre-heated oven for 60-70 minutes until a skewer inserted into cake's centre comes out clean.

Pecan Pie

    12 oz (300g) shortcrust pastry (see p. 66)
    3 eggs, beaten
    1 tablespoon (15ml) single cream
    6 oz (150g) soft brown sugar
    5 fl oz (125ml) maple syrup
    2 oz (50g) soft margarine
    1 teaspoon (5ml) vanilla essence
    6 oz (150g) pecan nuts, halved

Pre-heat oven to 220°C/425°F/Gas 7. Roll out the pastry to fit an 8 in (20cm) flan tin. Beat all ingredients except nuts together. Put half of nuts into flan case and spoon filling over. Place rest of nuts on top. Bake in pre-heated oven for 10 minutes. Reduce heat to 160°C/325°F/Gas 3 and cook for a further 45 minutes.

Pumpkin Pie

12 oz (300g) shortcrust pastry (see p. 66)
1 lb (400g) pumpkin, cubed
milk
2 eggs, separated
1 tablespoon (15ml) golden syrup
1 teaspoon (5ml) ground ginger
1 teaspoon (5ml) cinnamon
sprinkling of nutmeg

Pre-heat oven to 190°C/375°F/Gas 5. Cook the pumpkin in a little milk until tender (approximately 15 minutes). Remove pumpkin from milk and purée. Roll out the pastry to fit an 8 in (20cm) flan dish. Beat together all ingredients except egg whites and nutmeg. Beat egg whites until stiff and fold into the mixture, then spoon this into the pastry case and sprinkle with a little nutmeg. Bake in pre-heated oven for 30 minutes.

Treacle Tart

12 oz (300g) shortcrust pastry (see p. 66)
5 tablespoons (75ml) golden syrup
1 tablespoon (15ml) black treacle
2 oz (50g) ground almonds
3 oz (75g) fresh white breadcrumbs
grated rind of 1 lemon and 1 tablespoon (15ml) juice
1 egg, beaten
3 tablespoons (45ml) double cream

Pre-heat oven to 190°C/375°F/Gas 5. Roll out pastry to fit an 8 in (20cm) flan tin. Beat rest of ingredients together and pour into pastry case. Bake in pre-heated oven for 30 minutes.

Custard Tart

> 12 oz (300g) shortcrust pastry (see p. 66)
> 10 fl oz (250ml) milk
> 2 tablespoons (30ml) caster sugar
> 3 eggs, beaten
> 1 tablespoon (15ml) cream
> sprinkling of nutmeg

Pre-heat oven to 190°C/375°F/Gas 5. Use pastry to line an 8 in (20cm) flan tin. Prick pastry base all over with a fork, then line with greaseproof paper and weigh down with coins. Bake in pre-heated oven for 15 minutes. Remove paper and coins. To make custard, bring milk and sugar to the boil, pour on to beaten eggs (beat whilst adding milk), pour mixture back into saucepan and bring back to boil, stirring continuously. Take off heat and stir in cream, pour into flan case and sprinkle with nutmeg. Bake at the same temperature for 15-20 minutes until custard has set and is brown on top.

Chocolate Brownies

> 6 oz (150g) plain chocolate, melted
> 4 oz (100g) soft margarine
> 8 oz (200g) soft brown sugar
> 1 teaspoon (5ml) vanilla essence
> 2 eggs, beaten
> 6 oz (150g) wholemeal plain flour
> 4 oz (100g) raisins
> 2 oz (50g) nuts, chopped

Pre-heat oven to 180°C/350°F/Gas 4. Beat all ingredients together. Spoon into a greased, lined 11 x 7 in (28 x 8cm) baking tin. Bake in pre-heated oven for 30 minutes.

Stewed Fruit

1 lb (400g) rhubarb, gooseberries or blackberries,
   washed
2 tablespoons (30ml) sugar
2 tablespoons (30ml) water

Choose your fruit and prepare accordingly. For rhubarb, trim
off ends and chop roughly. For gooseberries, you need to trim
off both ends. Blackberries need no preparation.

Put all ingredients in a pan and cook gently for 15 minutes
until soft. Serve with custard or ice cream. As a contrast to the
soft fruit, I sometimes also serve some crunchy biscuits with
this.

Stewed fruit can be used as the basis of other desserts, like the
following:

FRUIT FOOL

Purée the stewed fruit and measure how much purée you
have. Add an equal amount of thick custard or whipped
cream (or a mixture of both). Stir and spoon into glasses. Chill
before serving. Again, this is very nice served with crunchy
biscuits.

FRUIT BRULE

Place the stewed fruit (no need to purée for this dish) in the
bottom of individual ramekins or a soufflé dish. Whip some
double cream and spoon enough over to cover the fruit. Now
cover the cream with caster or brown sugar. Put under a hot
grill and cook until sugar browns and bubbles. Leave to cool
before serving.

Rock Cakes

    8 oz (200g) wholemeal flour
    ½ teaspoon (2.5ml) mixed spice
    4 oz (100g) soft margarine or butter
    grated rind of half a lemon
    4 oz (100g) demerara sugar
    4 oz (100g) mixed dried fruit
    1 egg, beaten
    1 tablespoon (15ml) milk

Pre-heat oven to 200°C/400°F/Gas 6. Using an electric mixer, mix the flour, spice and margarine or butter. Stir in other ingredients. Place in heaps on a greased baking tray (makes 8-12, depending on size). Bake in pre-heated oven for 15- 20 minutes until brown.

Note
You can also use this recipe to make **Ginger Cakes** by substituting 2 oz (50g) chopped stoned dates and 2 oz (50g) chopped stem ginger for the mixed dried fruit.

Almond Slices

    8 oz (200g) self-raising flour
    4 oz (100g) sugar
    1 teaspoon (5ml) ground cinnamon
    6 oz (150g) unsalted butter
    1 egg, beaten
    2 oz (50g) flaked almonds
    1 oz (25g) preserving sugar

Pre-heat oven to 190°C/375°F/Gas 5. Sift flour, sugar and cinnamon into a bowl and mix with butter until you have a crumb mixture. Add 1 tablespoon (15ml) egg and knead to a dough. Roll out to fit an 11 x 7 in (28 x 18cm) tin. Brush with egg and sprinkle with flaked almonds and sugar. Bake in pre-heated oven for 25-30 minutes. Cool for 5 minutes, then cut into 12 slices.

Carrot Cake

This cake is not just for rabbits! I have always found it to be a very popular recipe with my friends.

8 oz (200g) wholemeal flour
1 teaspoon (5ml) ground ginger
1 teaspoon (5ml) nutmeg
1 teaspoon (5ml) baking powder
4 oz (100g) soft margarine or butter
4 oz (100g) brown sugar
4 oz (100g) runny honey
8 oz (200g) carrots, peeled and grated

Pre-heat oven to 180°C/350°F/Gas 4. Beat together all ingredients except honey and carrots, then stir these in. Spoon into a lined 1 lb (400g) loaf tin. Bake in pre-heated oven for 60-70 minutes until a skewer put into the cake's centre comes out clean. The cake can be decorated with orange icing if you wish – just mix 3 oz (75g) sifted icing sugar with 1 tablespoon (15ml) warm orange juice and then spoon over top of cake.

Raisin Slices

4 oz (100g) soft margarine
4 oz (100g) soft brown sugar
3 eggs, beaten
6 oz (150g) wholemeal self-raising flour
4 oz (100g) raisins
1 teaspoon (5ml) ground cinnamon
2 tablespoons (30ml) preserving sugar

Pre-heat oven to 180°C/350°F/Gas 4. Beat all ingredients together except preserving sugar. Spoon into a greased, lined 11 x 7 in (28 x 18cm) baking tin. Sprinkle with preserving sugar. Bake in pre-heated oven for 35 minutes. Cut into 15 slices.

Gingerbread

1 tablespoon (15ml) golden syrup
6 tablespoons (90ml) black treacle
3 tablespoons (45ml) molasses sugar
4 oz (100g) soft margarine
8 oz (200g) plain brown flour
2 teaspoons (10ml) baking powder
1 teaspoon (5ml) ground ginger
pinch of mixed spice
2 eggs, beaten
½ teaspoon (3ml) bicarbonate of soda
5 fl oz (125ml) milk

Pre-heat oven to 160°C/325°F/Gas 3. Melt syrup, treacle, sugar and margarine together. Mix in all dry ingredients except bicarbonate of soda. Beat in eggs. Dissolve bicarbonate of soda in milk and add to mixture. Stir well. Put in a greased, lined 2 lb (800g) loaf tin. Bake in pre-heated oven for 90 minutes. If this is wrapped in foil when cool and kept, it goes lovely and sticky!

Flapjacks

4 oz (100g) soft margarine
4 tablespoons (60ml) golden syrup
1 tablespoon (15ml) soft brown sugar
1 tablespoon (15ml) raisins
8 oz (200g) muesli
4 oz (100g) oats

Pre-heat oven to 150°C/300°F/Gas 2. Melt margarine, syrup and sugar. Mix in all other ingredients. Put in a greased and lined 11 x 7 in (28 x 18cm) baking tin. Bake in pre-heated oven for 45 minutes. Divide into 12.

Apple Cake

8 oz (200g) cooking apples, peeled, cored and chopped
8 oz (200g) mixed dried fruit
6 oz (150g) soft brown sugar
5 fl oz (125ml) Guinness
12 oz (300g) self-raising flour
1 tablespoon (15ml) mixed spice
6 oz (150g) soft margarine
1 egg, beaten
1 tablespoon (15ml) preserving sugar

Mix the apples with the dried fruit, sugar and Guinness. Let stand overnight. Pre-heat oven to 160°C/325°F/Gas 5. Sift the flour and spice together and rub in the margarine. Stir into the apple mixture with the egg. Put into a greased and lined 8 in (20cm), deep cake tin. Sprinkle with preserving sugar. Bake in pre-heated oven for 90 minutes.

Country Cake

6 oz (150g) soft margarine
3 oz (75g) soft brown sugar
3 eggs, beaten
4 tablespoons (60ml) runny honey
9 oz (225g) wholemeal self-raising flour
1 teaspoon (5ml) baking powder
1 teaspoon (5ml) cinnamon
2 oz (50g) chopped mixed nuts
4 oz (100g) cream cheese
2 oz (50g) icing sugar
2 teaspoons (10ml) coffee essence
sprinkling of toasted mixed nuts

Pre-heat oven to 180°C/350°F/Gas 4. Beat together all ingredients except cream cheese, icing sugar, coffee essence and toasted mixed nuts. Put in a greased, lined 8 in (20cm), deep cake tin. Bake in pre-heated oven for 45 minutes. When cool, beat together cream cheese, icing sugar and coffee essence. Spread over top of cake and sprinkle with toasted mixed nuts.

Apple Pudding

 2 dessert apples, cored and sliced
 2 oz (50g) soft brown sugar
 2 oz (50g) margarine
 1 egg, beaten
 2 oz (50g) self-raising flour
 2 oz (50g) raisins

Pre-heat oven to 190°C/375°F/Gas 5. Pile the sliced apples into a greased ovenproof dish. Mix together the sugar and margarine until creamy. Add the egg a little at a time, beating well. Then stir in the flour. The mixture should fall off the spoon quite easily (you can add a little milk if it seems very stiff). Stir in the raisins and spoon the mixture over the apples. Bake in pre-heated oven for 40 minutes, until risen and brown. Wonderful served hot with ice cream!

Apple and Date Slices

 1 lb (400g) cooking apples, cored and chopped
 4 oz (100g) dates, chopped
 2 oz (50g) walnuts, chopped
 4 oz (100g) wholemeal self-raising flour
 4 oz (100g) brown sugar
 1 tablespoon (15ml) honey
 1 tablespoon (15ml) margarine
 1 egg, beaten

Pre-heat oven to 200°C/400°F/Gas 6. Beat all ingredients together. Place in a greased and lined 8 in (20cm) flan tin. Bake in pre-heated oven for 25-30 minutes, until brown and risen. Leave to cool and then cut into slices – see how long you can manage to keep them in a cake tin!

Muesli Bars

    4 oz (100g) margarine
    4 oz (100g) brown sugar
    4 oz (100g) wholemeal self-raising flour
    4 oz (100g) muesli
    1 tablespoon (15ml) molasses sugar
    pinch of nutmeg

Pre-heat oven to 180°C/350°F/Gas 4. Melt margarine and
then stir in all other ingredients. Spread over a greased and
lined 11 x 7 in (28 x 18cm) baking tin. Cook in pre-heated
oven for 12-15 minutes, until risen. Cool and cut into bars.
These are very good for lunch boxes.

Hazelnut and Apple Pudding

    2 dessert apples, cored and sliced
    1 oz (25g) butter, melted
    1 tablespoon (15ml) runny honey
    1 oz (25g) wholemeal flour
    1 tablespoon (15ml) demerara sugar
    2 tablespoons (30ml) Greek yoghurt
    2 tablespoons (30ml) chopped hazelnuts

Pre-heat oven to 180°C/350°F/Gas 4. Pile apples into an
ovenproof dish. Mix all other ingredients together and spoon
over apples. Cook in pre-heated oven for 15-20 minutes, until
bubbling and brown.

Coconut Fairies

    1 egg white, beaten
    2 oz (50g) brown sugar
    3 oz (75g) dessicated coconut
    few drops of almond essence

Pre-heat oven to 160°C/325°F/Gas 3. Beat together the egg
white and sugar until stiff. Stir in coconut and almond
essence. Place in mounds on a baking tray and cook in
pre-heated oven for 30 minutes, until brown.

Peanut Cookies

   4 oz (100g) margarine
   4 oz (100g) brown sugar
   1 egg, beaten
   4 oz (100g) wholemeal self-raising flour
   2 tablespoons (30ml) peanut butter
   2 oz (50g) unsalted peanuts, roughly chopped

Pre-heat oven to 180°C/350°F/Gas 4. Mix together the margarine and sugar. Beat in the egg and then stir in the flour. Mix in the peanut butter and peanuts. Take pieces of the mixture and roll into little balls. Squash and put on a greased and lined baking tray. Cook in pre-heated oven for 15-20 minutes, until golden brown.

Banana Muffins
Makes 9 large or 18 small muffins

   10 oz (250g) self-raising flour
   pinch of salt
   1 oz (25g) soft brown sugar
   10 fl oz (250ml) milk
   1 egg, beaten
   2 bananas, chopped

Pre-heat oven to 180°C/350°F/Gas 4. Mix flour, salt and sugar together. Beat milk and egg together and mix into dry ingredients. Stir in bananas, but do not overmix. Put into muffin cases, half-filling each. Bake in pre-heated oven for 20-25 minutes, depending on size of muffin cases.

Banoffee Pie

This is one of those very wicked desserts that is always loved by everyone.

10 oz (250g) butter, melted
8 oz (200g) ginger biscuits, crumbled
16-oz (400-g) can condensed milk
2 bananas, sliced

Mix 4 oz (100g) butter and biscuits together. Line a 7 in (17cm) flan tin with foil and then press biscuit mixture into base of tin. Put rest of butter and condensed milk into a pan, bring to boil and simmer for 5 minutes, then leave to cool. Put half of bananas in flan case. When toffee mixture has cooled, beat well and spread over banana. Place remaining banana on top and chill. Serve with cream.

Fudgy Banana Pudding

2 bananas, sliced
4 oz (100g) muscovado sugar
1 tablespoon (15ml) water
4 oz (100g) dates, chopped
2 oz (50g) walnuts, chopped
5 fl oz (125ml) double cream

Place the bananas in two pudding bowls. Boil the sugar and water together to produce a syrupy caramel. Add the remaining ingredients and boil again for 1-2 minutes to produce a rich fudgy sauce. Pour over bananas and leave to set.

Chocolate Pots

> 1 tablespoon (15ml) cornflour
> 8 fl oz (200ml) milk
> 2 oz (50g) plain chocolate
> 2 tablespoons (30ml) caster sugar
> few drops of vanilla essence
> 1 chocolate flake, crumbled

Blend cornflour with a little of the milk. Break the chocolate into squares and melt in the remaining milk with the sugar. Pour the melted mixture onto the cornflour and then return this mixture to the heat. Stirring all the time, cook until mixture thickens. Remove from heat and add vanilla essence. Put into 2 ramekins. Chill until set and decorate with crumbled flake before serving.

Chocolate Crunch

> 4 oz (100g) plain chocolate
> 3 tablespoons (45ml) strong black coffee
> 1 tablespoon (15ml) butter
> 2 oz (50g) crumbled biscuits, cornflakes or nuts

Gently heat together the chocolate, coffee and butter. Remove from heat and stir in the 'crunch' you have chosen. Place in little mounds on greaseproof paper and chill overnight. Can be eaten as sweets or served crumbled over ice cream.

Chocolate Mousse

> 2 oz (50g) plain chocolate
> 2 eggs, separated
> 1 chocolate flake, crumbled

Melt the chocolate in a bowl over some hot water. Beat the egg yolks and add to the chocolate. Whisk the egg whites until stiff and then stir into the chocolate mixture. Fold in the flake, reserving a little for serving. Divide mousse into 2 ramekins, and before serving sprinkle with remaining flake.

Fruit 'n' Nut Ice

6 oz (150g) unsalted cashews or almonds, finely
  chopped
10 fl oz (250ml) fruit purée (see p. 181)
2 tablespoons (30ml) runny honey
2 oz (50g) raisins

Blend together the nuts and purée. Mix in honey and freeze
for 2 hours. Fork through ice and stir in raisins. Freeze again
until solid. Transfer to refrigerator for 20 minutes before
serving.

Brown Bread Ice Cream

3 oz (75g) wholemeal breadcrumbs
3 oz (75g) muscovado sugar
2 eggs, separated
1 tablespoon (15ml) runny honey
15 fl oz (375ml) double cream

Stir-fry the breadcrumbs and sugar together in a non-stick
frying pan until sugar melts. Beat the egg yolks into the honey.
Whisk the egg whites until stiff, then beat the cream until stiff.
Gently fold all ingredients together. Cover and freeze for one
hour. Stir through to break up ice. Freeze again until firm.
Transfer to the refrigerator 30 minutes before you wish to
serve.

Ecclefechan Tart

12 oz (300g) shortcrust pastry (see p. 66)
4 oz (100g) butter
4 oz (100g) soft brown sugar
2 eggs, beaten
1 tablespoon (15ml) white wine vinegar
6 oz (150g) mixed dried fruit
2 oz (50g) walnuts, chopped

Pre-heat oven to 190°C/375°F/Gas 5. Roll out the pastry to fit an 8 in (20cm) flan tin. Prick base all over with a fork. Place a sheet of greaseproof paper inside and some coins. Bake in pre-heated oven for 15 minutes. Remove paper and coins. Cream together the butter and sugar and beat in the eggs. Stir in the rest of ingredients. Spoon into the pastry and level the top. Bake at the same temperature for another 25-30 minutes until filling is brown and firm to the touch.

Mud Pie

It may have a very strange name – the dark chocolate does remind me of sludge! However, if you think that banoffee pie is a wicked dessert, just wait until you try this one!

12 oz (300g) shortcrust pastry (see p. 66)
15 fl oz (375ml) double cream
8 oz (200g) marshmallows
8 oz (200g) plain chocolate, broken into cubes

Pre-heat oven to 220°C/425°F/Gas 7. Roll out the pastry to fit an 8 in (20cm) flan tin. Prick base all over with a fork. Put a sheet of greaseproof paper on top and weigh down with coins. Bake in pre-heated oven for 15 minutes. Remove paper and coins and cook for a further 10 minutes. Remove from oven and leave to cool. Put 10 fl oz (250ml) of cream in a saucepan with marshmallows and chocolate and heat gently, whilst stirring until melted. Leave to cool for 45 minutes. Spoon half of mixture into pastry case. Whip remaining cream and then stir into the rest of the chocolate mixture. Spread over the chocolate mixture in the pastry. Refrigerate overnight.

Index